Never Regret the Pain:
Loving and Losing a Bipolar Spouse

Sel Erder Yackley

Never Regret the Pain:
Loving and Losing a Bipolar Spouse

Helm Publishing

For information, address:
Helm Publishing
3923 Seward Ave.
Rockford, IL 61108
815-398-4660
www.publishersdrive.com

ISBN 0-9769193-5-4
Printed in the United States of America

Library of Congress Cataloging in Publication Data

Yackley, Sel Erder, 1939-
Never regret the pain: loving and losing a bipolar spouse / Sel Erder
Yackley.
p. cm.
ISBN 0-9769193-5-4 (pbk. : alk. paper)1.
Yackley, Francis Xavier, 1936-1986. 2. Manic depressive persons--
Illinois--Biography. 3. Judges--Illinois--Biography. I. Title.
RC516.Y33 2006
616.89'50092--dc22
[B]
2006011141

REVIEWS

<u>Today's Chicago Woman</u> July 2006 The Book Nook,
For an inspirational read in Never Regret the Pain: Loving and Losing a Bipolar Spouse, former Chicago Tribune writer Sel Erder Yackley recalls the devastating effect her husband's mental illness had on her family, the lessons she learned and how she moved on to find peace.

<u>Chicago Suburban Woman</u> and
<u>Suburban Woman North Shore,</u> July/August 2006, Book Corner
Sel's book is a page-turner...Frank, adamantly opposed to the death penalty, became clinically depressed following a murder trial where he was compelled by law to impose such a sentence. The experience was traumatic, his behavior became erratic and his depression deepened.

<u>TurkofAmerica</u>, August 2006
Sel Erder Yackley, originally from Istanbul, has written a fast-paced, easy-to-read memoir, giving hope to people who have had tragedies in life. Now living in Chicago, Mrs. Yackley lectures on mental health issues, is active in international organizations and organizes educational tours to Turkey.

<u>Turkish Digest</u>, May 29, 2006
Turkish-born, U.S-educated Sel Erder Yackley has added another feat to her long list of accomplishments. Her memoirs "Never Regret the Pain: Loving and Losing a Bipolar Spouse," is in its second printing by Helm Publishing. Affectionately known as "Mama Turk" in Chicago for her nurturing nature, Mrs. Yackley has written an excellent book that educates, informs and comforts the reader. Turks are anxious to have it translated and published in Turkey.

This book is a sobering testament to the effects of Bipolar Disorder on an entire family. I recommend it to anyone who would like to know more about this potentially devastating illness and its social manifestations.
--Burgess Wilson, M.D, Department of Psychiatry, Rush University Medical Center

I bought a copy in Barbara's Bookstore here in the hospital. I was so moved by the story I am recommending it to many nurses here to read.
--Janet Cahill, Director, Professional Practice and Development at Northwestern Memorial Hospital

I was very much impressed with Sel's writing. Her journalistic background shines through. She frames the story well, keeps the narrative moving, and includes various kinds of anecdotes. I really think it will help people who face comparable situations.
--Stephen Kinzer, author <u>Overthrow: America's Century of Regime Change from Hawaii to Iraq</u>

Congratulations on writing such a compelling and <u>important </u>book. I really think it should be made into a movie, whether on the big screen or TV. I applaud your courage and that of your children for allowing such a holistic understanding to emerge. You are one <u>special </u>lady and have made a tremendous contribution to understanding the world of a family with a bipolar member. Bless you for expressing the sentiment, "Never Regret the Pain." We take from life what comes our way and retain in our souls the positive sunshine as fuel for our life journey.
--Barb Argumedo, Ph.D., Educational Change Agent

Spent the greater part of last evening racing through your book, weeping copiously at times. A remarkable story, by a remarkable woman! The book is terrific and will help many, many people, I think.
--Virginia Bolen, Attorney-at-Law, formerly of San Francisco

Thanks so much for sharing your life with us. The cover, the chapter beginning quotes, mention of those we knew in Ottawa all tie in to make it truly an inspiring book. It's bringing out so many different emotions.
--Billy Staff, retired teacher, Vandalia, Illinois

Frank was a textbook case of bipolar disorder; his symptoms and the disease course are remarkably consistent with what I've read and professionally encountered when working with individuals with bipolar disorder. It is among the more serious of mental illnesses and its unpredictable nature is incredibly hard on the family. Hopefully, we will make strides in its treatment; in the meantime, families and patients will just have to hang in there. Thanks for your candor, openness, and willingness to disclose these issues.
--Denise Lash, Ph.D. in Psychology, New Mexico

Acknowledgement

The Chicago Law Bulletin *printed an article I wrote in October 2001 on the John Whitehead murder trial, which illustrated the psychological effects of the death penalty on the circuit judge who imposed it. The judge was my late husband Francis Xavier Yackley. Friends urged me to expand on it. In February 2002, three of us former Chicago Tribune colleagues took a road trip to Cincinnati, Ohio, to visit a friend. While Susan Hilkevitch drove, Linda Andrews was adamant about helping me with an outline of a memoir. She had just finished writing a book on how to choose a college major and knew every author needed a push. "Begin by writing a few hours a day. Put down whatever comes to mind," she urged me.*

My first inclination was to write an autobiographical book beginning with my Turkish ancestors for my children to share with their children. Thanks to Enid Powell, the leader of the Chicago-based Breakthru Writing Workshop, I realized my most compelling experience was loving and living with a bipolar spouse. After reading several chapters, Enid steered me in the right direction – writing my own story of coping, surviving, and thriving. She and fellow writers patiently critiqued the work in progress. Author and attorney Mary Hutchins Reed, specializing in intellectual property, gave me solid editorial and legal advice.

The week I spent at the Iowa Writers Festival in June 2004 made me zero in on the right focus. Instructor James McKean and classmates guided me in choosing the title, urging me to persevere and get it published.

D. Clancy, a close friend and published author, caught my grammatical errors, punctuation inconsistencies and helped with chapter headings.

Numerous friends and fellow writers deserve credit for keeping me on track. I am also grateful to my children whose help was indispensable. My daughter refreshed my memory on several facts and polished the final version. My sons, cautious and worried at first, praised the work and allowed me to share their trials and secrets in these pages.

Dianne Helm, my publisher, who saw the benefit of sharing my experience with families in pain and was resolute about the book's marketing and distribution.

I owe the biggest thanks to long-time friend and retired Chicago Tribune *editor Marion Purcelli who cheered me on when I was ready to give up. Without compensation or complaint, she read every word, discussed the content, style, details of descriptions, and chapter sequence. Since she knew Frank, and had shared some of my pain, our collaboration became therapeutic for both of us.*

With love to my children John, Ayla and Joe.
With gratitude to my parents and husband.

Bipolar Disorder, also known as manic depression, is a mood disorder, which includes depression as well as mania. Symptoms of hyperactivity can progress to agitation, irritability, paranoia, and grandiosity. Like depression, it is believed bipolar illness is caused by a chemical imbalance in the brain.

Two million Americans are diagnosed each year with bipolar disorder, a no-fault brain disease characterized by severe shifts in mood, energy, and ability to function. Bipolar people may experience mood swings from euphoria or irritability to sadness and hopelessness, then back again, with periods of normal moods in between.

Table of Contents

Prologue

Chapter

> **"We must embrace pain and burn it as fuel for our journey."**
> – Kenji Miyazawa

Prologue

I had no idea which direction our lives would go when I married Frank. As reporters, we were happy to be witnessing history while eking out a living. We were attracted to each other because we were opposites. He was quiet, private, and mysterious. I was bubbly, sociable, and an open book. Frank's indecisiveness and contradictions were exciting challenges for me. I was adventurous and adaptable – having left my native land of Turkey at age 16 and assimilated into American society. I had chosen journalism as a career, even though English was my second language. Above all, like most other young women in the 1960s, I wanted a good marriage and children. I was ready to support my husband's career ambitions whatever the cost to my professional aspirations.

Little did I know Frank's ambitions would take us to such heights. He was destined to become a well-known public figure, an admired prosecutor, and a highly respected judge.

He would also fall into the depths of despair as he suffered manic depression in his mid-40s. He opposed capital punishment but followed the law instead of his personal principles by sentencing a murderer to death, thus unraveling his own life as well as ours.

This is my true story, but in certain instances, for my own reasons, I have changed the names of some characters. This book is about loving and living with a bipolar husband and dealing with the circumstances of his death. It is about how my three children and I struggled and coped, took our fate in stride, pulled closer together, and eagerly accepted support from friends.

I hope my story inspires and sustains families in similar pain, educates the public about bipolar disorder, and promotes more research for better treatment of mental illness.

Recognized as brain diseases and perhaps caused by viral infections, schizophrenia and bipolar disorders are treatable just like other chronic ailments.

I fervently urge people to seek treatment. The earlier one gets help, the more likely a better outcome.

"Lie you easy, dream you light."
– A.E. Housman

1- Lie You Easy

I heard my name blaring from the loud speaker in O'Hare airport's international terminal and ran to the ticket counter, questions rushing through my mind. What could have happened? Who besides Frank knows which airline I'm taking?

I had completed every detail at home before leaving for my flight to Turkey to spend three weeks with my children and parents. As was their custom most summers, John, 16, Ayla, 14, and Joe, 12, were visiting their grandparents and my sister, Nil, who traveled from Germany to join them for six weeks every summer. The sun, the sea and my mother's comforting arms would surely lift my spirits and prepare me for the uncertainty of our future as a family.

While waiting for the boarding call, I reflected on all that had happened during the past four months of 1986, and was grateful that the children were spared the anguish of watching the mounting difficulties between their father and me. I took comfort knowing they were on the Sea of Marmara in the warmth of their grandparents and their aunt's love. Nil considered my children her own and took an active part in their lives.

The Yackley children enjoyed submersion in the Turkish culture and language. While they were happily ensconced for the summer, I toiled away in my public relations work and tried to avoid thinking about my now chaotic 20-year-long marriage.

Three months previously, Frank had moved into an apartment because he said he needed space. That morning he had called to wish me a good trip. He was in a decent mood and said he was going to see his therapist before going to work. He promised to take care of our cat and keep an eye on our house in Ottawa, Illinois, including picking the peaches as they ripened on the tree in our backyard.

Breathless, I arrived at the ticket counter and was told by an agent to call our family friend Peg Breslin. I ran to the pay phone. Peg answered on the first ring and in a somber but calm voice said, "I'm afraid there has been a terrible accident. Frank has been shot."

Stunned, I gripped the receiver, unable to speak.

"Sel, Sel, are you there?" Peg shouted.

"Yes, I am here," I whispered. "Tell me, is he alive?"

"I'm afraid not," she answered. "The sheriff discovered his body at the shooting range about an hour ago."

Shaking, I spoke my first thought: "He killed himself, didn't he?"

"They're investigating all that," she said. "My husband is on his way to the airport to bring you home. We were lucky Carolyn Andrews overheard you tell the driver you were flying KLM when she took you to the shuttle stop."

I held my hand on my throat to keep from sobbing. Dazed, I went to fetch my bags from the young woman with whom I had carried on an animated conversation during the previous hour. She looked at me with a curious expression.

2

"I need to go back home," I said, with a thick tongue that made it difficult for me to talk. I mumbled, "My husband has been shot." The shock on her face was probably mirroring mine as I began to realize the enormity of the tragedy I was about to face.

How could I break the news to our children? I was to bring them back to Ottawa so they could jump into their dad's arms after several months' absence. Frank often said he could not live without the children. Now, the children had to live without him. The sudden death of their athletic, brilliant father was inconceivable. The possibility it was suicide added an awful dimension to our loss. There were countless questions that needed to be answered:

Had we failed him or had he betrayed us?

How could we face the people of this small town where everyone knew and respected him?

How could I comfort, love, and support my children when I was so shaken?

How could I be a mother and a father to them with no family here?

Where would I turn?

Despite my jumbled thoughts, I explained my situation to the concerned KLM agents as they led me to a desk with a telephone in the back office. I first called my brother-in-law in Germany who tracked down my sister and told her to expect my call. Then I dialed a series of numbers and waited anxiously for the connection to Erdek, Turkey, where it was almost midnight. I prayed that my sister, not one of the children, would answer the phone. "Hello," I said. From the tone of my voice, Nil knew something terrible had happened. I sobbed as I told her I would not be on the flight that night and that Frank was dead.

"I am sure it was suicide," I said. "Please break the news gently to the children. Tell them I love them and I will call back in an hour."

I spent the next hour at the KLM desk, calling Frank's family and friends. I first talked to Betty Yackley, Frank's sister-in-law, a psychologist who had known him since he was 13 years old.

"Oh no. No. No!" she screamed into the mouthpiece. When she heard my sobs, she apologized and offered to call Frank's three sisters and brother. She said she would leave Naperville, Illinois, Frank's hometown, right away and get to Ottawa before I would get there.

"I'm staying with you as long as you need me," she added.

Next I called Frank's namesake cousin, then his long-time friend Larry Lorenz, the best man at our wedding. Each call sucked the wind out of my lungs and depleted the tears from my eyes.

More than ever, I wished I were in Erdek, hugging and kissing and crying with my children. I shuddered when I thought about how they would react to this devastating news without me. I wondered if they would want to fly home right away or if they would need some time to adjust and mourn.

With a broken heart, I called back and talked to each one. I told them that Frank was found dead at a shooting range and that I thought it was suicide. Each expressed concern about my state of mind and tried to comfort me.

"You decide," I told them. "Shall I delay the funeral two or three days so you can get back here? Or shall I go ahead with the burial, fly to Turkey to be with you for a few weeks, then have a memorial service when we return?"

Two to one, they chose the second option. Joe, the youngest, was outvoted.

Driving back to Ottawa, John Breslin and I tried to make sense of what had happened that day. We knew Frank had an aversion to firearms. "Guns scare me. I don't like being anywhere near them," he had told us.

This death was so sudden, so unthinkable that our small town of Ottawa came to a standstill. In a matter of seconds, the Circuit

Court had lost one of its most popular judges, and I had become a widow.

I returned to find my two-story brick home brightly lit and full of friends who hugged me, cried with me, and tried to comfort me with food, wine, and sedatives. Neighbors walked in and out. Betty and I talked late into the night since sleep escaped me. Early the next morning she drove me to the funeral home so I could pick out a casket.

The bullet had gone through the right temple, shattered Frank's brain, and tore through his large brown eyes. Very little was left of his handsome face. The funeral director, a close friend, spent 24 hours restructuring his head and face to make him look as if he were sleeping peacefully.

The undertaker remembered Frank's love of sports and literature, so he placed a basketball and a book of poems by A. E. Housman in his casket. I decided against a wake, knowing it would be too hard for me to maintain my composure without our children at my side.

Because Frank was a private man, I asked for his casket to be closed. Peg took care of the funeral arrangements at St. Columba Church, and her husband John, Frank's law-school classmate, handled the financial essentials, taking care of the paperwork for life insurance, social security, and pension plans.

At first, there had been confusion about the cause of death. The sheriff and the coroner wanted to rule out foul play but were puzzled about the bullet's point of entry. Having witnessed Frank sign arrest warrants and other legal documents with his left hand, they did not realize he was ambidextrous until friends told them Frank ate, played basketball, and threw a football with his right hand. That's when the cause of death was determined to be from a self-inflicted gunshot wound. Blood tests showed no sign of drugs in his system. Everyone learned the truth from banner headlines in the LaSalle County newspapers, but they knew nothing about his devastating illness, especially since he had hidden it from colleagues to mute any questions about his performance on the judge's bench.

During the two days between Frank's death and the funeral, I could not sleep, eat, think, concentrate, or talk coherently. I was angry. I was sad. I was so lost. I felt like a ghost. I did not know what I would do nor how my children would cope, but I knew that to keep Frank's memory alive and his legacy intact, I had to be strong for my children and dignified for the community.

Still in shock, Frank's older brother and three sisters drove to Ottawa from Naperville on that hot, humid August Wednesday in 1986. Sitting by his casket, we cried, prayed and reminisced about Frank's childhood and college days. We spoke of the early years of our marriage, family reunions, and his exceptional career.

My heart was heavy with grief and my muscles ached from fatigue as I approached the casket to bid farewell to the love of my life, to my man of contradictions: a brilliant scholar with little self-confidence; a tough prosecutor but compassionate judge; a good husband who reveled in solitude; the athlete, the poet, the storyteller, and the loving father.

An *Ottawa Daily Times* photographer volunteered to take pictures of Frank in his casket so the children could see their father one last time to help them accept the finality of his death. Looking at the photographs of the funeral service would also reinforce the fact that Frank was much loved and respected.

"This may help bring closure," people said. I knew better. There would always be a void. We were at the threshold of an unfamiliar life without him.

Fellow circuit judges were pallbearers. The standing-room-only church service had the largest attendance of any funeral in the county's recent history. Even though Frank had left the Catholic Church, the priest knew him and delivered a beautiful eulogy.

The powerful voices of the choir accompanied by the organ pierced my heart as they sang "Let There Be Peace On Earth" and "Ave Maria." Dressed in black, sobbing like a child, I was overwhelmed with a range of emotions: anger, relief, gratitude, and loneliness. I was 46 years old with three children under the age of 17; being a widow was never in my plans. Frank took such good care of himself physically that I teased him about outliving me. Even though we had separated, I had still hoped to throw a surprise 50th birthday party for him that fall and dreamed of a 25th wedding anniversary bash organized by our children in five years.

The procession to the cemetery consisted of 200 cars. I was in a fog from exhaustion, lack of sleep, and mental anguish but I did not want the prayers to end. Eventually the casket was lowered into the ground, rain-soaked dirt and flowers thrown over it. Choked with sorrow, I turned and walked away as my tears mixed with the warm summer rain.

At age 49, Frank's final resting place was under a cherry tree with branches spreading out in all directions.

Loveliest of Trees

Loveliest of trees, the cherry now
Is hung with bloom along the bough,
And stands about the woodland ride
Wearing white for Eastertide.

Now, of my threescore years and ten,
Twenty will not come again,
And take from seventy springs a score,
It only leaves me fifty more.

And since to look at things in bloom
Fifty springs are little room,
About the woodlands I will go
To see the cherry hung with snow.

Frank, obsessed with A.E. Housman whose philosophy centered on pessimism and defeat, often recited his poetry and praised him for writing "with such compelling grace that he made darkness seem desirable."

The cherry tree under which we buried Frank was in the well-tended Oakwood Cemetery, a few steps from the grave of a neighbor's son, Tim Vegrzyn. Shy, quiet, and studious, Tim often played basketball with Frank. His mother, Nancy, having heard about the basketball in Frank's coffin said, as she gave me a tearful hug: "Maybe they will shoot baskets together in heaven."

Tim had just passed his CPA exam and accepted a well-paying job in Chicago when his girlfriend broke up with him. When Nancy woke up early on a warm morning in March 1984, she noticed Tim's bed was not slept in. By early afternoon everyone in the neighborhood was on the lookout. Around 5 p.m. two young boys came upon Tim's body in a wooded area by the Illinois River where many of us used to hike. Everyone suspected foul play. Frank, preparing to preside over another murder trial, said the less he knew about it the better.

Within hours, however, the coroner ruled the death a suicide. This news totally shocked and saddened Frank.

"Tim had so much to live for. Why did he take such a desperate step?" he asked.

Two years later, at Frank's funeral, a neighbor, a successful accountant, expressed similar thoughts. According to his wife, he wondered why would Frank, such an intelligent and accomplished person, take his own life? Alas, three years after Frank's funeral, hooked up a hose to his car's exhaust pipe, placed the nozzle inside, got in, turned on the ignition and ended his own life.

When I think of Frank, Tim, the neighbor, and others who have taken their lives, I remember a quote by the Roman philosopher Seneca, who lived in the first century:

"Death is the release from all pain and complete cessation, beyond which our suffering cannot extend. It will return us to that condition of tranquility which we had enjoyed before we were born. Should anyone mourn the deceased, then he must also mourn the unborn."

"Death is our marriage with Eternity."
– Mevlana Jalaluddin Rumi

2 - Death Is Eternity

During the next few weeks, I asked a lot of questions, listened to friends and law enforcement officers, and searched for clues in Frank's apartment, where he had moved in the spring. After the memorial service, dozens of friends and colleagues told me about their final contact with Frank on August 4, 1986. Like putting together a puzzle, I came up with a pretty clear picture of what happened during his final days.

Frank had gone target shooting at a range on Highway 6 east of the town of LaSalle in the weeks before his death. This should have been the last place Frank would go. It was owned and operated by a low-level criminal Frank had prosecuted when he was district attorney for illegal weapons' trafficking and tax evasion. Frank told the owner he had purchased 17 acres of land on the Illinois-Michigan Canal (which was true) and wanted to teach our boys how to hunt (which was a lie). Once he learned how to shoot, he methodically planned his death.

After calling to wish me a good trip, Frank kept his biweekly appointment with his psychiatrist where he was calm, content, and glad he had coped well with ten tough days on the bench in Chicago. Downstate judges were sometimes assigned to Chicago to help with the backlog. I later learned that some patients with severe depression often appear markedly improved just before committing suicide.

Arriving at the Ottawa courthouse at about 9 a.m., Frank made small talk with the clerks and lawyers and speculated about the upcoming Chicago Bears' football season. The morning call went swiftly. He told his clerk he would return at 1:15 p.m., drove to his apartment for lunch, chatted amiably with a neighbor, and greeted the mailman.

He entered his apartment, browsed through the mail, and tore open an envelope from Mendota Community Hospital that contained a $1,100 bill for recent cosmetic surgery to repair an old incision on the top of his head. The incision had split open during a recent basketball game, making the scar worse.

He emptied his wallet on the kitchen counter and probably looked at the children's photos he had lovingly matted, framed, and placed on shelves next to his cherished books and busts of Lincoln and Churchill. Then he drove 12 miles to the shooting range.

Frank bought 50 rounds of ammunition, went to the furthest target, and turned off the car, but left the key in the ignition. He walked down a knoll, took aim at the bull's eye, and shot one bullet after another. Loading and reloading the .45 caliber gun I can see him crying, tears soaking his crisp white shirt. He shot 48 bullets, leaving only two in the gun's barrel. Putting the nozzle to his right temple, he pulled the trigger.

Forty-nine years old, my husband was consumed forever by darkness as the 49th bullet ended his life.

Two young men walking through the shooting range discovered the body an hour later, and Coroner Marion Osborn and Sheriff's Deputy Herb Klein, two family friends, rushed to the site to identify it. Marion told me Herb fainted when he realized who was lying there lifeless.

Years later I came across Frank's well-worn book of *Peter's Quotations*, a collection of quotes he often incorporated into his speeches and writings. Thumbing through it, I found check marks on the margins of a variety of subjects. Disturbing to me were the double asterisks he put next to quotes on suicide.

"A tendency to self-destruction seems to be inherent in the overdeveloped human brain." – A.T W. Simeons

"The thought of suicide is great consolation; with its help you can get through many a bad night." – Friedrich Nietzsche

"I have had just about all I can take of myself."– S.N. Behrman

"Suicide was naturally the consistent course dictated by the logical intellect. (Is suicide the ultimate sincerity? There seems to be no way to refute the logic of suicide but by the illogic of instinct.) – William James

"Men just don't seem to jump off the bridge for big reasons; they usually do so for little ones." – W. H. Ferry

After reading these, I asked myself why I had not discovered this book and recognized Frank's fixation with death. Why hadn't I seen where these morbid thoughts would take him? If I had, what could I have done? There was little information readily available about depression and suicide in the early 1980s, and I had taken

Frank to the doctor the minute he had told me his suicidal thoughts. Was there more I should have done?

Frank's burial completed my final obligation to him. Now I needed to concentrate on my children's well-being. They were 7,000 miles away and anxiously awaiting my arrival. Flying across the Atlantic Ocean on August 6, 1986, I thought about what Frank told me:

"You have been a supportive partner, a good wife, and a great mother to the kids. I could not have come this far without you."

His praises always made me feel appreciated, especially because they were unsolicited and expressed frequently. He often repeated that he had achieved his aspirations with my help. "You are confident, and you are strong," he had said. "If anything happens to me, you will be fine."

The humming of the jet engines hypnotized me after the plane left U.S. airspace. I prayed for better days, I dug deep into my past for strength. I explored my life, starting at the beginning.

As I traveled back to the city of my birth, I asked myself if I was somehow destined to be alone on this plane, in this world, grieving the loss of my husband and marriage.

I was born in late December 1939 in Istanbul, the imperial capital of the Ottomans that had slipped into decay during the decades after World War One. Water was frequently cut, and rain mixed with snow had turned the streets into rivers of mud.

Determined that her children claim Istanbul as their birthplace, Selma had left the industrial town of Eskisehir in central Turkey with her 2-year-old daughter Nil to stay with her mother before giving birth to her second child. Her husband Nezihi followed, and the family huddled into a large room in the matriarch Sudiye Budak's grand Ottoman-era apartment.

Selma tried to banish her apprehension about Hitler and the war in nearby Europe. "Only four more days before the start of a new decade," she thought as she touched her protruding belly. She checked to make sure the covers were tight around Nil sleeping in her crib and crawled into bed shortly before midnight. She smiled thinking of the new baby due in three weeks. An hour after she drifted into a restless sleep, Selma was jolted and jerked out of bed. Nezihi also awakened, reached for the lights and soon realized the electricity was cut off. After another quick jolt, they knew they were experiencing the tremors of an earthquake far away.

"But why the pain?" Selma cried as she doubled over. Then she realized: "I am going to have the baby."

Everyone in the Budak household was awake and standing with candles in their hands. They took cover in doorways and prayed for the rattling and shaking to stop. Nezihi grabbed a blanket, eased Selma's arms into her coat, draped his own over his shoulders, and ran into the cold air to hail whatever vehicle he could find. Selma entrusted Nil to her mother and boarded a horse carriage, the only available transportation, hoping the ride would not be too bumpy on the cobblestone streets. The two arrived at the German Hospital, and in less than an hour, welcomed into this world a frail little girl, just under six pounds. We later learned that on that same day, December 28, 1939, more than 35,000 Turks died in Erzincan, 700 kilometers east of Istanbul, during one of the worst earthquakes of the 20th century.

Born prematurely in the middle of a natural disaster, I had no name for a few weeks. Finally, a poet friend, who had named Selma's first born after the river Nile, suggested the unusual name of Sel, which means "flood" in Turkish. "When the Nile floods, it brings prosperity to its riverbanks," he said.

Forty-six years later on this flight half way around the world, I wondered how many more disasters I was destined to overcome. With Frank's suicide, my life had changed forever, and I was determined to triumph over this adversity.

The Turkish resort where my children spent their summers was a close-knit community of families who returned year after year. They were genuinely shocked and saddened at the news of Frank's death, but did not know how to comfort the children.

Because suicide is considered to be a shameful act in Muslim nations, my mother told everyone Frank was shot to death. This encouraged speculation about the reasons. Was the mafia somehow involved? Had someone Frank had sentenced to prison taken revenge? Not discussing their father's suicide confused the children at first and delayed their healing process. They felt uneasy about keeping a secret in Turkey while having to adjust to the truth when they returned to Illinois.

I had to be truthful with the children. I reminded them that their father's life had been a roller coaster the last three years and, though he had moved out of the family home, we were keenly aware of his pain. I brought the photographs from the funeral and a letter Frank wrote to the children the week before my departure. Though he often signed his notes with his initials FXY, this letter was different. Dated July 28, 1986, and neatly typed on his judge's stationery, it was signed "Dad."

Dear John, Joe and Ayla,

Long time, no see – especially you, John. I have been working in Chicago for the last 10 days. At times like these, when I am alone and have time on my hands, I think of the three of you constantly. You are all I care about in the world. All parents think their kids are great, but I truly believe the three of you are special. I believe each of you will do very fine things in life and each in very different ways. I not only love you but I admire each of you so much. I look up to you as one would ordinarily do only with older persons.

As you know, I have suffered from personal, inner problems of a very heavy sort for the last three years, so that life has not been the same for me. The greatest pain is to think how lovely things might have been in the home between you three and me. I would do many things differently if I had it to do over again – I would spend more time with each of you. Still, I love the way you have turned out, and I would not change anything about any of you. Please think of me and remember that you are all I care about.

Enough of that. The Bears are in London to play the Cowboys. They should be wonderful again this year.

Sel will bring this to Erdek with her.

I love each of you dearer than my own soul.

Dad

This letter was a comfort to the children, their father's good-bye. But it had been a concern to me before his death.

"Is this a suicide note or a call for help?" I asked his sister in-law Betty, who had tried to counsel him. She didn't think so.

"Don't worry, Frank doesn't have the guts to kill himself," she said.

Peg and John Breslin, the only friends who knew Frank's inner struggles, were not alarmed, either. I had left a copy of the letter with Frank's psychiatrist, Dr. Joseph Chuprevich, knowing Frank had an appointment with him that week. I did not hear from him.

How could we all have been so wrong?

"No one is perfect until you fall in love with him."
– Andy Rooney

3 - No One Is Perfect

I met Frank in July 1963 when I reported for my first day of work at United Press International in Chicago. Frank later told me he was intrigued from the moment he saw me. He and fellow reporter Larry Lorenz eyed me up and down when I entered the newsroom.

"She's got a great body," Larry told Frank.

"I like her face," Frank said. "I'd like to get to know her."

UPI had moved its Broadcast Wire Service from Manhattan to Chicago in the late 1950s and needed young reporters who were quick and competent and willing to work on a meager salary. The broadcast department, providing hourly news updates for 1,700 UPI radio and television subscribers, had hired only one other woman before I arrived, just 23 years old and with a master's degree from Northwestern University's Medill School of Journalism.

Our office was on an upper floor of the old Kemper Insurance Building, located across the Chicago River from the Lyric Opera House at the corner of Madison and Canal streets. In those days this corner marked the eastern boundary of a seamy area, Chicago's Skid Row.

I commuted from suburban Evanston where I shared an affordable attic apartment with Joanna Hawkins of Birmingham, Alabama, who was getting a doctorate degree in theater from Northwestern. Overjoyed that I now had a steady income, I spent my first paycheck ($175 for two weeks' work) on an a-line skirt, a silky long-sleeve blouse, a pair of black pumps, and a handbag from Andrew Geller's store on Michigan Avenue.

Larry and Frank, graduates of Marquette University in Milwaukee and now roommates, finished their military obligations before they had taken jobs at UPI the previous year. Frank was hired first and, on his recommendation, Larry started three months later. My only contact with them was during the shift change. I usually arrived at 8 a.m. when both were tired, sleepy, and hungry from working the overnight shift. I found Larry forward and talkative, while Frank was shy and introverted. Handing over the day's roster, Larry would joke around while Frank would inform me of breaking news and about the stories that needed to be updated.

The war in Vietnam was accelerating, and I had to read pages of news off Teletype machines from Reuters and other international news services. My job was to reword them concisely and precisely for use by radio and television stations. The writing needed to be crisp, in the present tense, and spelled out phonetically so announcers would not stumble over foreign names or phrases.

Working for UPI fit nicely into my plans to eventually transfer to Istanbul to be closer to my family. Getting paid for doing something that kept me informed, educated, and enlightened was a bonus. We worked in a large room, crackling with Teletype machines. News reporters were at one end of the newsroom, and the broadcast-wire desks formed a circle at the other end.

A year after I was hired, UPI moved its offices to a brand-new building on Michigan Avenue, across the street from the *Chicago Tribune*. Billy Goat's Tavern, a hangout for the staff of the *Tribune* and the city's other dailies – *Chicago's American, The Daily News* and *The Sun-Times* – were in the lower level of our building. At any given time we would join the conversation with cartoonist Bill Mauldin of the *Sun-Times*, columnist Mike Royko of the *Daily News*, or the sports writer Dave Condon of the Tribune. Royko and Condon were often engaged in deep discussion on the merits of the Cubs versus the White Sox.

My most unforgettable day at UPI was President John F. Kennedy's Dallas visit and his assassination shortly after noon on Friday, November 22, 1963. UPI had scooped the competition by accident. Our White House correspondent was using the only phone available in the press car just behind the president's limousine when shots were fired from the old Texas School Book Depository near the grassy knoll area. As other reporters grappled for the phone, he dictated the incident to the news desk in New York, which quickly wired it to UPI desks throughout the world. I was standing by the Teletype machine in the Chicago bureau when the bells went off: "FLASH!" Co-workers later said they remembered the expression of pain on my face as I read the news.

"The shock, disbelief, and grief etched on your face as you read the Teletype report reflected the immensity of this tragedy," veteran reporter Everett Irwin told me.

In the chaos that followed, phones rang incessantly, typewriters clicked, and Teletype machines spit out reams of paper. We were on automatic pilot writing, rewriting, and updating the story. Working overtime, none of us wanted to go home. Larry and a few others came in to help. Around 8 p.m. several of us went down to Billy Goat's Tavern to bury our sorrows. Larry had called Frank at their apartment to invite him along, but he said he wanted to sleep so that he'd be alert for the onslaught of news when he came in for the midnight shift. I found it odd that a newsman could sleep at a time like this. Since I had little contact with Frank, I didn't give more thought to his lack of emotion in the face of such a tragedy.

Larry and I bonded after this incident and comforted each other as we mourned the loss of our beloved president. We dated for a few months, often talking about J.F.K, the Camelot that was never to be, our opposition to the war in Vietnam, politics, and work.

Frank, in the meantime, was asking Larry a lot of questions about me and finally made up his mind to ask me out after learning Larry and I had chosen to stay friends. At a New Year's Eve party at the home of a colleague, Frank found a spot on the couch next to me and started an animated, witty conversation. He listened attentively as I talked about my childhood, my time as an exchange student in Arizona, my college days at Arizona State and Northwestern. He knew a lot about the Ottoman Empire and the Republic of Turkey. At the stroke of midnight, he leaned over and gave me a gentle, hesitant, but lingering kiss. It was daring and endearing at the same time, and it marked the beginning of our on-again off-again courtship.

Dating Frank did not sit well with co-workers, especially some of the married men who were always looking to flirt. Propositioning female writers was a habit of some of the hard-drinking, womanizing newsmen. They were eager to tell me about Frank's shortcomings, like the time he skipped three weekends of duty in the Coast Guard Reserves for which he was later pulled away from UPI to serve six weeks of active duty in Duluth, Minnesota. I considered it a youthful indiscretion.

Office romances are always complicated, but Frank and I were working different shifts and decided we would continue dating. I soon fell in love. His intelligence, wit, good looks, and humility captivated me. He was intriguing and deep. He read biographies, talked about the Civil War, told anecdotes about presidents and prime ministers, recited poetry and quoted Carl Sandburg on Abraham Lincoln. I was learning so much from him. He was fascinating, funny, and handsome.

The only member of his family to finish college, Frank went on to earn a master's degree in English literature from the University of Connecticut. He had taught at Loyola University of the South in New Orleans and joined the Coast Guard Reserves before starting work at UPI. I asked him why a college instructor would choose to become a reporter. He said he would have stayed in academia if he had chosen history instead of literature.

"Literature is too abstract," he said. "The news business gives you an opportunity to experience history."

An avid reader with a photographic memory, he would dispense information freely and with a "gee-whiz" attitude that never questioned others' knowledge on the subject. He admitted he was emotionally undemonstrative, but said he was trying to change that. I was never bored around him. Not knowing what he would say or do from one day to the next was exciting to me. His key virtues were being honest and non-judgmental, and I was attracted to his unpretentious manner and gentlemanly reserve.

Looking back on those years, I now wonder what it was that attracted me to Frank. Our backgrounds had little in common. I came from a highly educated family. My great grandfather, a four-star general in charge of the Ottoman infantry during the reign of Sultan Abdul Hamid II, lived with his family on the grounds of Dolmabahce Palace on the Bosphorus strait in Istanbul. My mother went to French schools and became a teacher, then a journalist. My father studied mechanical engineering in Germany and had supervisory positions in several sugar factories before becoming the general manager of the Ankara electric and gas company. Both spoke three languages. My older sister Nil was studying architecture in Germany. She and I were educated in private schools. Ours was a close-knit family.

By contrast, Frank was the youngest of seven children. One of his sisters died from the flu in infancy. His parents were devout Catholics who struggled to put food on the table during the Great Depression. His father, Johann Jaegli, left school before the sixth grade in a village called Wittisheim near Strasbourg in Alsace, under German control at the time, and enlisted in Kaiser's army. He emigrated to the United States in 1913, the first in his family to do so. Upon arrival at the Port of New York in Ellis Island, it was suggested that Johann change his name to the more Anglicized "John Yackley."

John eventually made his way to the Midwest and found work at the Burlington Railroad in Aurora, Illinois. He spoke no English for several years, and once he learned it, he had a thick German accent. He said he was refused American citizenship twice because of anti-German sentiment in the United States after World War One. In 1923 he married Augusta Berger who was born on Chicago's South Side and was of Alsatian heritage. She had lost her mother at age 13 and helped raise five younger siblings.

"If I had known I would have seven children, I would have never married," Augusta said. She was 39 and her husband was 49 in 1936 when Frank was born, the youngest in their brood.

John and Augusta saved enough money in the 1920s to purchase a three-bedroom home in Naperville, Illinois, which they furnished with Augusta's earnings as a telephone operator. They even had a Model T-Ford with a rumble seat for a short while. Gusty, as Frank's mother was called, was an avid reader who spent most of her free time in later years at the public library. John lost his job at the Burlington Railroad during the Great Depression and was lucky to find work at the Chicago stockyards and packinghouses, carrying heavy slabs of meat on his back. He drank heavily after finishing his grueling shifts. "Had to," he told his children later in life. "Long wait for the train back to Naperville."

"We had so little money that some days we ate oatmeal for breakfast, lunch, and dinner," Frank said. Their small home afforded unusual sleeping arrangements. While growing up Frankie and his older brother Johnny slept in the same bed with their father whose "whiskers scratched my face and snoring kept me awake," Frank related to me later. The two oldest sisters had a room and the younger sister slept with Gusty.

Frank took his sweet time before introducing me to his parents. He said he seldom brought home his girlfriends because he was embarrassed about his Dad's thick German accent and his mother's matronly looks.

"Everything is old, out of date, and cluttered around here," he said. He also explained that his sister Jo Ann had psychological problems that kept her from realizing her dream of becoming a nun. Their fraternal uncle, Crazy George, was a drifter in the United States and France and died when a train hit him. Frank speculated that he might have committed suicide.

"Who would want to marry into this crazy family?" he once said.

I thought I would. In those days I did not know mental illness was genetic. I loved Frank and felt comfortable around his family, though I found them aloof. Still, I was bothered by his trepidation toward commitment. He had been engaged twice before he met me. He explained he had no business, while in graduate school, proposing to Jeannie, a model.

"Her mother was anxious to see Jeannie settle down. She put me in such an awkward position that I ended up asking her to marry me," he said. Within weeks he realized his mistake and broke off the engagement. Later he met a sweet, quiet Filipino-American named Wing, who was "a good Catholic." But she was culturally very different, and her family was suffocating in its closeness.

I saw Frank's indecisiveness as a minor personality flaw. There was adventure and drama in everything we did together:

23

going on bike trips in Wisconsin, canoeing down the Fox River in Illinois, and hiking up New Hampshire's White Mountains.

Years later I realized that what I thought was adventure and drama was really distress and instability. Our ill-equipped hiking escapade in New Hampshire almost resulted in both of us suffering from hypothermia. Our capsized canoe in the Fox River cost us our cameras and other gear.

I soon forgot about my plans to return to Turkey and marry a Turk as Frank and I began to talk about a future together. I had convinced my parents that he was the right person. During a visit out West in 1965 to see Dr. and Mrs. Joseph Reavley, the family who hosted me when I was a high school exchange student, Frank purchased a beautiful engagement ring with two perfect diamonds flanking a deep blue sapphire.

After our return from Arizona, Frank changed his mind about proposing. We had just finished a simple meal at his apartment when he told me he was confused about our relationship. The blue velvet box with our engagement ring was tucked away in a drawer. I was crushed.

"What kind of courtship is this? Why are you tormenting me?" I said. Tears welling up, I grabbed my coat and scarf and ran out of his apartment, slamming the door behind me.

I decided this was the end of our relationship and that I had to get far away. Thank God for friends. My Arizona State University dorm-mate, who was teaching in Brazil, had invited me to travel with her in the southern part of South America. So early in January 1966, eager to see the world and get away from Frank at the office, I took four weeks off without pay and flew to Rio de Janeiro.

I had succeeded in escaping Chicago's bitter cold and warming my body and soul in temperatures hovering around 100 degrees. Barbara Beuckman and I became girls from Ipanema in Rio de Janeiro, relaxing and partying before we took off on a six-seat plane that landed on a short grassy strip by the Iguassu Falls

24

bordering Paraguay. We witnessed extreme poverty in Asuncion, Paraguay; mingled with rich concertgoers in Santiago, Chile; had heated discussions about U.S. foreign policy with friends in Montevideo, Uruguay; and stayed in the home of a doctor in Porto Alegro, Brazil, a family with whom I still correspond. The trip lifted my spirits.

"Having a wonderful time. Latin men are great," I wrote on a postcard I mailed to a fellow Northwestern graduate and co-worker, Stu Camen on the sports desk. The postcard found its way into Frank's hands.

The card triggered something in Frank who decided to meet me at the airport upon my return. I was surprised to see him with my winter coat over his arm and a sheepish look on his face as I walked through the gate at O'Hare. I was no good at playing games so I thanked him for his trouble and asked why Stu had not picked me up. "I volunteered," he said as he put his arms around me and gave me a long, loving squeeze. "Will you go to dinner with me tonight? Or are you too tired?"

I told him I would rather go home and unpack, but that I would take a rain check.

Quickly he said, "How about tomorrow night?"

He picked me up promptly at 7 p.m. the next night and took me to dinner at Kon-Tiki Ports, a romantic restaurant in the old Sheraton Hotel on Michigan Avenue. He was trying to listen to my tales about Chile, Uruguay, Paraguay, Brazil, and Argentina, but I could tell he was anxious to talk himself. He fidgeted with the miniature paper umbrella as he sipped a Polynesian drink. Suddenly, he reached into his pocket and took out the blue velvet box. "Let's get hitched," he said.

"Let's do it right away. Before you change your mind." Then he confessed, "If we don't do it now, we will have to wait until after Lent."

We are where we should have been a year ago, I thought. But I was overjoyed and believed only true love would have brought us to this point. I agreed to marry him, but said he had to ask for and get my parents' permission.

My mother kept, and gave back to me years later, Frank's letter asking for my hand. It took my parents three months, several more letters, and a couple of phone calls before they gave their blessing. Across the United States, Mom and Dad Reavley, as I called my host parents in Arizona, were relieved to hear that Frank had finally proposed.

Born in a Muslim but secular country, I had very little religious training and considered myself an agnostic. I agreed to get married in a Catholic church and told Frank he could raise our children as Catholics. He was accepting of others' beliefs or lack of them so he never asked me to convert or attend church with him. Before we were married, the priest at Our Lady of Mount Carmel Church in Chicago gave me some religious instruction and, somewhat to our surprise, permission to take birth control pills for a few years.

The road to our wedding was rocky at times. Frank became more unpredictable, agreeing to do something, and then changing his mind. He had second thoughts about settling down even though he had promised himself he would be married before he turned 30. One weekend we were sanding and varnishing a chest of drawers in my apartment when he suddenly began crying. I had never seen Frank lose his composure, and I had no idea what to do. My pulse quickened, and I took the sandpaper out of his hand. "Frank, look at me," I pleaded. "Tell me what is bothering you. Why are you so miserable?" I was preparing myself for one more change of heart. If he hadn't been crying, I would have kicked him out of my apartment right then.

In between sobs he apologized. He said he really did love me and wanted to spend the rest of his life with me. He was under a lot of pressure, and his stomach hurt all the time.

"I just don't know what is wrong with me," he said. Never suspecting psychological problems, I urged him to see an internist.

The first one said he should avoid acidic foods and that stress could cause an ulcer. His stomach aches persisted, so he sought a second opinion. Following numerous tests, this doctor told him his stomach was not producing enough acid and that he should consume acidic foods. Frank had baffled even the doctors.

> **"The head never rules the heart,**
> **but just becomes its partner in crime."**
> – Mignon McLaughlin

4 - I Do, I Do

On a cool, overcast Saturday, April 30, 1966, Frank and I exchanged marriage vows at Our Lady of Mount Carmel Church on Belmont Avenue in Chicago. Frank was 29 and I was 26. Larry Lorenz, Frank's best man, said he was surprised Frank had finally tied the knot.

My American dad Joseph Reavley walked me down the aisle, having driven all the way from Phoenix with Mom and a carload of gifts from their friends in Arizona. Frank's ailing father, my parents, and my sister could not attend. It was too far for them to travel.

I wore a borrowed fitted-bodice white gown with a long train. My maid of honor and bridesmaid wore dresses in turquoise, my favorite color. A UPI photographer friend took the pictures. Our boss Bill Ferguson and his wife Betty hosted a lovely reception in their Evanston home attended by 100 friends and Frank's family members. The wedding cake was cut, the presents opened, the bouquet caught by an anxious girlfriend, and the garter grabbed by Stu Camen, and we were on our way to the airport.

It should have been the happiest day of our lives, but Frank was tense and pre-occupied. I knew he did not like traveling and grudgingly had agreed to spend our honeymoon in Fort Lauderdale, Florida. Thinking back, his pre-occupation might have been triggered by his concern about our inexperience in lovemaking. He was a good Catholic, and I came from a conservative culture where premarital sex was taboo. We had been loving and intimate but had not gone all the way. That week was the blind leading the blind. Frank was awkward. I pretended not to notice. I figured we were in love and had a lifetime to improve our sex life. My husband, however, looked at our love life gloomily. On our flight back, he took a Harold Monro poem out of his wallet and read it to me. He later matted, framed, and hung it on our bedroom wall.

From "Midnight Lamentation"

We are too much alone;
What can we do
To make our bodies one:
You, me; I, you?

We are most nearly born
Of one same kind;
We have the same delight,
The same true mind.
Must we then part, we part:
Is there no way
To keep a beating heart,
And light of day?

I cannot find a way
Through love and through:
I cannot reach beyond
Body, to you.
When you or I must go
Down evermore,
There'll be no more to say
But a locked door.

I was confused. I was unsure about what he was trying to tell me, whether I should be sad or happy. I tried to understand why he was so morbid at the threshold of our life together. So I decided the poem did not contain a secret meaning and that reading it to me was a reflection of his romanticism. After all, we were young, healthy, educated, and earning a decent living. We had similar, traditional values. We hoped to have children. He wanted four, though I thought two would be enough.

We began to build our life together by combining our few pieces of furniture and settling into a one-bedroom apartment with a dining room and an eat-in kitchen at 3400 North Lake Shore Drive. Our windows overlooked the alley so the rent was cheap at $125 a month. Like many other young couples, we were on a tight budget and had little money for extras. For recreation, we bought bikes at Sears and rode along the lake on weekends. In good weather I biked to work.

Frank organized touch football games on Sundays. We enjoyed free movies at the old Clark Theater using our press passes, which also afforded us swim privileges at the Olympic-size pool at the Sheraton. Some weekends we visited Frank's widowed mother in Naperville and Larry in Milwaukee as he pursued a Ph.D. in journalism at Marquette. Frank continued his Coast Guard Reserve duty one weekend a month and two weeks in the summer. We were happy with our normal, ordinary lives.

Eventually, I took a job at the *Chicago Tribune* and knew that Frank needed a change too. He said he was tired of UPI and Chicago and longed to live in a small town, idealizing his childhood days spent at the YMCA in Naperville, a town of 5,000 people when he was growing up. He envied his oldest brother Bob's life on a farm and his Catholic grade school classmates' stress-free existence in Naperville. He reminisced about his escapades with his brother John on the Des Plaines River in borrowed canoes, their pranks of rolling pumpkins down Main Street, or ordering by phone crazy-sounding pizzas from a parlor run by a guy they despised.

It had been five years since his last career change. He was itching for a new experience and spoke about wanting to move to "serene and beautiful New England." He had spent two years at the University of Connecticut in Storrs and missed the surrounding hills. Determined to find work there, and, with my full support, he flew to Hartford for a couple of interviews in southeastern Connecticut.

I found the idea of living in New England appealing. Having lived in Arizona and the Midwest, I would now get to know another part of my adopted country. Also, I had cousins near Boston and I would be closer to my family in Europe. In the dead of winter in 1967, I helped Frank pack most of his possessions in a recently purchased VW microbus and sent him on his way to a reporting job in Ansonia, Connecticut.

I submitted my resignation at the Tribune, sublet our apartment, and was ready to pack the furniture and supervise the movers before flying to Hartford in a few weeks. But Frank was miserable out East. Unlike Storrs, Ansonia was an industrial town. Frank hated the newspaper assignments –school board meetings and city council debates in cramped, overheated buildings.

"I can't stand the dark, dreary days here," he said soon after he arrived. When not working, he was trying to learn about local politics and meet key people.

"I haven't had time to look for a place to rent, or even unpack anything," he informed me. The microbus held his stereo, books, and other items of comfort, but he was living out of a suitcase in a small hotel room. Knowing how flustered Frank got when things did not go his way, I understood he was looking for a way out.

"If you are that miserable, why not come back to Chicago?" I asked him.

I explained my dilemma to the Tribune's Neighborhood News section editor, Russell MacFall, who graciously allowed me to keep my job. The renter reluctantly agreed to find another apartment. Frank told the publisher of the Ansonia paper he was sorry, but the job was not for him. He quickly repacked the VW and drove home, walking into my open arms on a cold, snowy January day. He kept kissing my face, my eyes and my neck, saying how glad he was to be back. This had been an expensive learning experience – we had spent our savings on the VW van, an impractical vehicle on Chicago's crowded streets – but Frank had found being a reporter in a small town was not for him.

Six weeks passed, and Frank could not find employment in Chicago. Discouraged by dead-end leads and suffering from cabin fever during the snowiest year on record, Frank became irritable and depressed. Why couldn't he get something with one of the four daily papers in Chicago? Even though my boss tried to help, a position at the conservative, non-union *Tribune* was unlikely since Frank had been a vice-president of the Wire Service Guild while working at UPI. *Chicago's American* hired him as vacation relief for a couple of weeks, but did not have a permanent opening. No reporting or editing positions were available at the *Daily News*. The *Sun-Times* was our last hope.

During these weeks I saw a depressed, impatient Frank. He was impulsive one day and compulsive the next. His need to be working was all-consuming. If he could not get a job with a major newspaper in Chicago, he said he would find a way to move us to a small town. This could mean yet another career for Frank.

After two months of anxious reflection, Frank finally shared with me his secret ambition: He had always wanted to go to law school but could not afford it.

"Instead of reporting the news, I want to make the news," he said. "I know I cannot work as a newsman in a small town so I have to find another way of accomplishing my goal."

We were lucky. I enjoyed my job at the *Tribune,* and it provided us with an adequate income, health insurance, and a nice circle of friends.

"Why don't you see if you can get into a law school?" I said. "We can live on what I earn."

Winter quarter was already in session, and most schools would not admit students until the fall. While he waited, Frank continued to look for a news job and was finally hired by the *Sun-Times.*

He was elated when Loyola University's law school offered him a full scholarship, starting in September. The first semester was difficult. Frank was going to school full-time while working at the *Sun-Times* part-time, often tempted by offers for full-time positions. Several times a week he threatened to quit school.

"Law school is like parachuting into the Bavarian Black Forest in pitch dark and trying to find my way out of the woods," he said. "And do you realize I am older than some of my professors?"

I kept telling him he was granted a full scholarship and had to finish at least this first term. Years later, he told our children he did not have the heart to quit law school after he caught me crying with frustration over his wavering.

During Christmas break that year, he sat at the typewriter and started writing a report for one of his classes and suddenly found inspiration in what he was doing. He quit working at the *Sun-Times* and devoted his energies to his studies for the next two and a half years. He was involved in Moot Court competitions and became a role model for younger classmates, often organizing study sessions. The close relationships he developed with his professors continued into his later years.

Frank wanted to rekindle some of his college memories and show me his stomping grounds in New England. So in June 1968 we packed our bicycles and camping gear in our van and embarked on a leisurely trip through Michigan, New York, Massachusetts, Vermont, and New Hampshire. I feared for my life on a climb to the top of the White Mountains in New Hampshire. Frank had hiked in these mountains while he was a graduate student at the University of Connecticut and said he knew his way. The fog, the rain, and the cold slowed and confused us. Suffering from a urinary tract infection, dressed improperly, and carrying little food, I had no business hiking in the White Mountains. Pure adrenaline eventually helped us find our way back to town. Frank later told me he was scared to death we might have wound up with hypothermia, a frequent occurrence in New Hampshire's mountain ridges.

It was after this trip in the fall of Frank's second year of law school that I became pregnant. I had already convinced him that we could manage work, school, and a baby. My parents had spent three months with my sister in Germany since my father's retirement and they wanted to see the United States and meet Frank. I was sure I could convince them to stay longer than the planned three months once they found out I was expecting their first grandchild.

"Of course, we will stay until the baby is born," said my mother. They ended up staying two years, getting along well with Frank. Mother's simple English was sufficient to communicate with Frank, and my father tried to talk to him in German. Frank learned a few Turkish words and phrases, which he flaunted with an imaginative sense of humor. When someone asked him how he was in Turkish, he would answer: "Aslan gibiyim," or "I'm like a lion." Every night he would ask my folks, "Whisky istiyor musunuz veya dondurma istiyor musunuz?" ("Would you like whisky or ice cream?") He would proceed to serve them with pomp and ceremony.

That winter I took my folks out West to meet my American parents with whom they got along beautifully. We showed them the Grand Canyon, Disneyland, Knott's Berry Farm, and the Pacific Ocean. When we returned to Chicago, my parents enjoyed visiting with some of our Turkish friends and taking advantage of Chicago's cultural offerings. I continued to work at the *Tribune,* and Frank studied hard.

On Bastille Day 1969, July 14, the day after my parents' 37th wedding anniversary, we welcomed a healthy, active boy into our midst. Frank was almost 33, and I was nearly 30. My parents loved taking care of their grandson John, making life easy for us. While Frank went to school and I was at work, my father pushed John's stroller on long walks along the lake and my mother cooked or sewed. On occasion she brought John downtown to modeling agencies for special catalog shoots and even a television commercial.

They stayed with us in that crowded one-bedroom apartment until after John's first birthday. John's crib was next to the sofa bed where they slept. The dining room had the television, giving us a chance to enjoy our whisky or ice cream after John fell asleep. Frank's typewriter and desk were in the corner of our bedroom where he could concentrate on his studies.

Throughout law school, Frank talked about wanting to go into public service. Following graduation and the bar exam, my parents helped us pack and move to Ottawa, Illinois, 80 miles southwest of the city. We chose Ottawa for several reasons, including its proximity to Chicago and the two Turkish couples we knew there. Frank's niece was raising horses in the country outside of Ottawa. On previous trips, we had met Peg Breslin's family who had been farming there for several generations. We had camped at nearby Starved Rock State Park. Besides, Ottawa was the seat for LaSalle County, and the state's attorney was a Democrat.

On August 1, 1970, we rented the upstairs apartment in a big house on tree-lined Congress Street in an old residential neighborhood on the east side of town. I loved the spacious, high-ceilinged converted apartment with three large bedrooms, two baths, a huge living room, a separate dining room, a large closed-in porch that ran the width of the house, and a garage. Nobody lived downstairs and the yard was full of tall oak and maple trees. It was a bargain at $140 a month.

By the end of August, my parents were ready to return to Turkey, but their airline tickets had expired. They had accumulated a great number of souvenirs and other possessions. My father wanted to see a little more of the world, so I researched the availability of cargo ships leaving from Chicago's Navy Pier. We found a Yugoslavian freighter that would take 18 passengers and travel through the St. Lawrence Seaway to the Atlantic; across the ocean and through the Gibraltar strait, and end of up in Rijeka in present-day Croatia. The trip would take 30 days and cost $300 per person including three meals a day. My mother thought 30 days on a ship would be boring, but my father was thrilled.

We packed two trunks and several suitcases and delivered Selma and Nezihi to the ship in early September 1970. They had a cabin as big as our old living room with two picture windows decorated with lace curtains. My mother had plenty of newspapers and books to read; my father was happy with his Atlas and the latest edition of the World Almanac. They had their backgammon set and *bejzik* boards, a French card game they enjoyed.

We met French- and German-speaking passengers on board, felt reassured that this had been a good choice, and waved them goodbye as the freighter pulled away.

Because of delayed cargo and harbor regulations, the trip took 60 days instead of 30 – much to my father's delight. Going through the Great Lakes and St. Lawrence Seaway and stopping in Milwaukee, Detroit, Toronto, Montreal, and Quebec was a great adventure. They disembarked in each harbor town and got to see friends on several occasions.

My father spent his days visiting with the crew, watching the loading and unloading of freight, while my mother read, knitted, talked to fellow passengers, and learned to relax. After crossing the Atlantic, they stopped at ports in Spain and Italy and disembarked in Yugoslavia. They then took the train to Hanover, Germany, to visit my sister and her husband. My father told anyone who would listen that this was the best trip of his life.

**"I belong to no organized political party:
I am a democrat."**
– Will Rogers

5 - Life in a Small Town

With a law degree now in hand, Frank finally realized his dream of living in a small town. He wanted to work in the public sector and especially for a Democratic state's attorney. There were few Democratic counties within 100 miles of Chicago in those days, but LaSalle County was the exception. We needed to be close to our friends in Chicago and family in Naperville. And most of all, we wanted to live in a scenic town with a YMCA so we could stay in shape (no one had heard of health clubs in the early 1970s).

Bob Richardson, a gregarious Irish-American, was serving his third term as state's attorney, having first been elected on President John F. Kennedy's coattails in 1960. LaSalle was a sleepy, rural county of 112,000 residents, managing with one prosecutor and two part-time assistants. Frank needed a full-time job and convinced Bob to persuade the county board to increase the state's attorney's budget so he could be hired. His beginning annual salary in 1970 was $7,000, nearly half of my wages as an editor at the *Chicago Tribune*. We reasoned that living in a small town would be less expensive and his earnings would increase as he proved his worth.

The setting was idyllic. Frank's office was in the 120-year-old sandstone courthouse four blocks from home. The grade school our children would attend was on the next block, and the YMCA was within walking distance, as were most stores. We awoke to the chirping of birds in our trees each morning.

We already knew people in Ottawa and had very friendly neighbors, many of them our age. Frank's legal career was launched with most of the professionals in the community impressed by him, his newspaper background, and his diligent work.

The challenge for me was to switch gears and become a full-time mother, managing a household on little income. It took me almost a year to adjust to my new lifestyle.

At age 34, Frank was thriving in his third career. But I felt useless, missing the excitement of the news business, mourning the loss of our vibrant big-city life, and bereft of a career of my own. To assuage my restlessness, I applied for a slot man's position at the local newspaper, the *Ottawa Daily Times*. The editor gave me a puzzled look and asked what a slot man did.

"He or she is responsible for assigning the re-writing of stories, editing the articles, and writing headlines," I told him.

He said the only thing they did with an article was proofread it for grammatical errors. "We print whatever the reporters turn in," he said.

Having learned from Frank's reporting experience in a small Connecticut town, I decided to forget about advancing my journalism career and looked elsewhere. I began substitute teaching at the junior high and high schools. Frank was supplementing our income by teaching criminal justice courses at the nearby community college and helping train state troopers at the Illinois Police Academy in suburban Lisle.

During the summer of 1971, the house in which we lived was sold to St. Columba Church as a residence for six nuns. We had to move. I had looked at a couple of homes before going to Turkey with John, and Frank purchased the three-story brick home across the street before I returned. That same year we caused some commotion among long-time Ottawa residents, as we became vocal activists on environmental issues. On one occasion we collected hundreds of signatures to stop the mayor from building a bridge at the end of our street in order to relieve 20 minutes of what he called rush-hour traffic on Main Street by the high school. There already was a bridge one block south accessing the east side to the rest of Ottawa.

Eventually, I learned to like my new hometown, especially as I discovered its historic significance. The area had been home to human beings since 8000 B.C.; Hopewellian, Woodland, and Mississippian Native American cultures thrived here. When it was incorporated in the mid-1830s, Ottawa was larger and more vibrant than Chicago, and in 1858 it was the site of one of the political debates between Abraham Lincoln and Stephen A. Douglas in a campaign for a U.S. Senate seat.

Frank, the history buff, became popular as he wrote historical articles for the Illinois Bar Journal, accepted speaking engagements, and participated on radio talk shows.

Our daughter, Ayla Jean, was born on New Year's Eve 1971, two and a half years after John. This time, instead of my parents, my younger cousin stayed with us in our new spacious home, auditing high school classes to improve her English and typing skills, while helping care for John and Ayla.

Few calls were coming in for substitute teaching, so I pursued another idea. I convinced the administrator of the Community Hospital of Ottawa to hire me as their part-time public relations director, even though few hospitals had PR departments in the early 1970s. He agreed they needed to improve their image because they had acquired property to build a modern facility along the Fox River east of town. One of my responsibilities was fundraising, another was establishing better relationships with the news media, and the third was communicating with the public. I also wrote and edited a monthly newsletter, designed to improve the morale of the staff. We had a different doctor write a column for each issue, and the administrator kept employees abreast of developments. We honored an outstanding staff member each month and had a classified section where people could sell items.

Because we had only one car, Frank biked to work and to the YMCA for noontime basketball games. The five-block ride would take him by the high school where students would be lingering before classes started. They would cheer or boo Frank, depending upon what had transpired at the courthouse that week.

One day he was pedaling his 1965 model three-gear Sears special faster than usual. He had on his pinstriped suit and highly polished shoes. His red tie was flying in the wind, and his briefcase was bouncing in the wire basket. All of a sudden his front tire hit a stone, and the bike came to a dead stop. As Frank flew over the handlebars, doing a summersault, he heard a roar of laughter, then applause and jeers.

"I felt like a fool as I picked myself off the pavement, brushed the dirt off my suit, and seeing that I had a flat tire, walked the bike the rest of the way to work," he told me when he got home. In those days Frank enjoyed laughing at himself. He continued to ride his bike to work until a new criminal justice center was built on Ottawa's north side.

In early 1973, I became pregnant for the third time, and my parents made their second trip across the ocean for another extended visit. Frank was making rapid strides in his legal career, becoming a highly respected and capable prosecutor. We were active in Democratic politics and were campaigning hard to get Bob Richardson elected circuit judge. Two weeks before the

41

election, Bob died of a massive heart attack. On October 17, 1973, the day Frank turned 37 he was sworn in as state's attorney. Two weeks later, on Halloween, we became the parents of yet another boy, Joseph Nezih Yackley.

Having been in the newspaper business, Frank had established a rapport with the press. He got along well with members of the bar association and the county board, often getting them to approve his requests for increased funding.

"He is persuasive, careful with our tax dollars, and effective in putting criminals behind bars," county board members said.

Confident and comfortable in this administrative position, Frank decided to run for a full four-year term as the county's chief prosecutor in 1976. To our surprise, publishers of the three LaSalle County daily newspapers, all Republican-owned, endorsed his candidacy, and he won the state's attorney's seat in a landslide. Frank's political campaigns were family affairs. At the height of the campaign in the summer months, which coincided with the 1976 Bicentennial Celebrations, all five of us put on matching baby blue T-shirts with the name "Yackley" encircling a navy-blue star and march in parades. We waved flags, handed out campaign buttons, and gave candy to children lined up along the parade route.

Once Frank had the brilliant idea that I should dig out my mandolin, from the fifth grade, and learn a patriotic song to play and sing at some of the political rallies we attended.

"That is so corny," I said to him, dismissing the idea quickly.

"But that's the whole point," he answered. "We want to do something corny, something different."

Anything for a vote, I thought as I dusted off years of neglect from the smooth shiny backside of the mandolin and turned it over. Some of the strings were missing, and the tuner knobs at its neck had turned yellow. Romantic Italian songs echoed in my head. As I pulled the pick from the base of the strings and heard that goose-bump-generating, screechy sound I came back to reality.

"I think you should find a banjo player," I told Frank. "Country western music will win you more votes."

He dropped the idea of musical accompaniment quickly, but took my alternative advice of entering all the running races in LaSalle County. These gave him great exposure.

While Frank continued his public service duties, I limited my public relations work to morning hours so that I would be home when the children returned from school. We led a peaceful, traditional small-town life as I took the children to basketball or swim team practice, and he picked them up in time for a simple dinner in our large kitchen. On the wall above the table hung a huge map of the world, giving us an opportunity to discuss geography, history, politics, poverty, and famine. Frank instructed the children about the Ottoman Empire, British colonies, the size and threat of the Soviet Union, divided Germany, and the contributions these countries made to the world's heritage.

Frank was attentive to the children's needs. He would roughhouse and watch an hour of television with them, bathe them, put them to bed, and read to them. He needed a minimum of eight hours of sleep, so he would go to bed early and get up around 5:30 a.m. to run and lift weights. My friend Carolyn Andrews would come by and the two of us would go on an easy jog before starting our day. The children would have a quick breakfast before leaving for school. Frank usually had a hearty breakfast at a diner across from the courthouse, often meeting other attorneys or law-enforcement officers.

During his years as state's attorney, Frank sent a lot of people to prison, but he also persuaded the judges he argued before to put other offenders on probation. He said, "As prosecutors, we help more people by accident than defense attorneys do on purpose." Many of the men he had prosecuted respected and admired him. They knew Frank sympathized with their problems, but that they had to pay for their crimes. One young man sent Frank a letter from prison that read, "Mr. Yackley, you've done me honor by sending me to jail. I have learnt (sic) to control my temper. I'm getting my high school diploma. Prison has been good for me."

Early in Frank's tenure, I brought Ayla with me to the courthouse after her preschool let out for the day. I sometimes took the children to see Frank at work. It was an opportunity to witness their father holding court in an august setting and, I thought, could perhaps serve as a lesson to them in the rights and wrongs of society. On this occasion, Frank was arguing in the sentencing phase of an embezzlement trial. "Pudgy" Harris was a good-looking, dark-haired guy – a well-known, small-time crook in Ottawa. After Frank finished his arguments, the judge committed Pudgy to two years in prison, then loudly slapped down his gavel. With a whimper, Ayla yanked her hand from mine and scampered off the spectator bench to run toward Pudgy, whose hands hung in cuffs before him. He stared down at her quizzically and she back up at him, then she opened her arms as if she wanted to be held. Pudgy, with shackled hands, lifted up her tiny frame and Ayla hugged his neck and pecked his cheek with a kiss before he set her back down and bailiffs marched him out of the room.

The spectators and officers of the court appeared aghast at Ayla's behavior, and I rushed for my daughter, fearing we had upset the decorum of the proceedings. I caught Frank's eye and saw he was smiling, visibly moved by the spontaneous act of humanity his four-year-old girl had just displayed. She was her father's daughter: Frank prosecuted the law with compassion.

He also had foresight. His was the first state's attorney's office outside of Cook County to hire female assistants. He then lobbied the state legislature to initiate a "shared-work" schedule to allow female prosecutors to work two and a half days a week so they could also raise their families.

Our favorite activity on Sundays was driving 15 miles to Starved Rock State Park to hike after a hearty breakfast in the lodge restaurant. The log-cabin lodge had a lobby as big as a basketball court with four fireplaces and a 30-foot ceiling.

Decorated with Native American art including statues, feathered headgears, colorful rugs, huge armchairs, card tables, and desks, the lodge provided a rustic getaway for visitors. After breakfast we would explore one or two of the 13 miles of well-marked trails that offered varying sights, smells, and sounds each season. Often our weekend guests were treated to Frank's storytelling about how in the 1760s, Chief Pontiac of Ottawa tribe upriver was slain by an Illiniwek Indian while attending a tribal council in southern Illinois. According to the legend, during one of the battles that subsequently occurred to avenge Pontiac's killing, a band of Illiniwek came under attack by the Potawatomi --- allies of the Ottawa --- sought refuge atop a 125-foot sandstone butte, and starved to death, giving the park its name.

Overlooking the Illinois River and one of the seven locks controlling the flow between Chicago and the Mississippi River, the butte commands a view of the Illinois Valley. The 2,500 acre park, created by glacial melt waters, was designated a state park by President Theodore Roosevelt and improved upon by the Civilian Conservation Corps as part of Franklin Roosevelt's efforts to create jobs during the Depression. As a big fan of Franklin Roosevelt, Frank often took this opportunity to tell our children about programs F.D.R. introduced in the 1930s.

We loved picnicking and hiking around the three state parks in LaSalle County with toddlers on our backs when they were little, and with them running ahead of us as they grew older. Our lives were balanced and full. Frank played basketball with fellow attorneys and founded the Samuel Johnson Society, a literary discussion group. I joined a volleyball team at the YMCA and played bridge a couple of times a month. We enjoyed visits by our Chicago friends and organized block parties.

Most popular of these parties were the "corn boils" in August where each family on our block could invite a dozen friends from outside the block. The week before the corn boil, several of Frank's friends, including the priest from St. Columba, would gather in our large basement to make sausage. Martin Serena, the Italian real-estate developer with the secret recipe, would bring a washtub full of already-seasoned ground pork, beef, and whatever else was in the concoction he created, along with a huge box of casings. He would set up the production line and yell out instructions on the fine art of stuffing. With the help of some metal utensils and a lot of wine, the guys would laugh, sing, and fill the casings with 50, 60, or 70 pounds of sausage. At the end of the evening I would fry up a couple dozen so that they could sample their creation and give it their stamp of approval.

The day before the party, neighbors and their kids would pick hundreds of ears of sweet corn from a friend's farm, and the wives would shuck them the next morning. Frank and the neighbors would then block off the street, arrange picnic tables provided by each family, hang a huge kettle on a tripod in our driveway, fill it with water from the garden hose, and then build a wood fire under it. Neighbors would bring enough cups, plates, and utensils as 100 or 150 guests arrived with the folding chairs and sports equipment for their children.

Older kids would organize touch football, soccer, or basketball games while adults would consume beer and wine as they waited for the water to boil and charcoal to turn red. Neighbors took turns cooking and serving, and we never ran out of food. Frank once convinced the Ottawa High School band to swing by our block during their practice session, play and march for us. He was in his element at such gatherings.

We also had our share of sad times. In a small town the death of a student in a car accident, the drowning of a child, or the drug addiction of a neighbor's teenager affected us as if a member of our own family was suffering.

One such tragic incident was the murder-suicide of an estranged couple. A violent man in his 30s had harassed, stalked, and threatened his ex-wife. Frank had issued injunctions to keep him away from her, but he never obeyed them. In those days there were no laws against stalking but Frank found enough evidence of brutality to have the husband arrested and sent to jail. Time and again, the man's parents would bail him out. After his final release from jail this angry man kidnapped his estranged wife and sped away through county roads. As the cops closed in on him, he pulled over, took out a gun, and shot and killed his wife before he turned it on himself. Distraught about not being able to prevent this tragedy, Frank went to the funeral and tried to comfort the victim's parents. For months he lived with the guilt of not having done enough.

Frank was active in the state's attorney association and attended meetings in Chicago and Springfield. He returned from one of these meetings wearing a new cashmere blazer and a tie. When I questioned him about this purchase, pointing out that he already had many blazers in his closet, he blew up. He hurled the glass of beer he was holding in his hand, which hit the wall across the family room and shattered into hundreds of pieces. I was shocked by his overreaction.

"Why do you always question my judgment?" he yelled. "I am the wage earner in this family, and I can buy what I want."

"I am the one who writes the checks and I know we cannot afford extravagant spending," I shouted back and marched out of the room leaving the mess for him to clean up. Later that night, he apologized, though he said he was not sorry for his purchase.

Halfway through his term as state's attorney, Frank decided to run for judge. The family worked hard once again campaigning as a team.

In November 1978, the people of the Third Judicial Circuit, which included LaSalle, Bureau, and Grundy Counties, elected him as their circuit court judge in a close three-way race. He was the Democratic nominee; his opponents, both born and raised in LaSalle County, split the Republican vote. Six years later, constituents overwhelmingly voted to retain Frank as their circuit court judge.

Within a couple of years after becoming a judge, Frank's seven colleagues selected him as chief judge, a leadership position that gave him an opportunity to bring about administrative changes and actively champion judicial reform with help from other chief judges in the statewide organization. He was in charge of assigning cases to other judges, selecting associate judges and training them, troubleshooting, and occasionally hearing cases. He seemed a lucky man. His career offered him challenges to right wrongs and to make a difference.

Although Frank loved being chief judge, he decided to step down after four years, fearing he would be perceived as monopolizing the position. He was also afraid of a contest. "I am too much of an egomaniac to lose to someone who might challenge me," he said.

I advised him against it. He was a good administrator and a good communicator. His colleagues had confidence in him, and the press was on his side. Why was Frank afraid of confrontation and competition?

It soon became clear he had made the wrong decision by stepping down, and instinctively, I braced myself for future hardships. The fellow who replaced him was Frank's nemesis, his unsuccessful opponent in the 1978 judicial election. He stayed in the chief judge's position for 10 years, until his retirement. The present chief judge has been in that position for more than a dozen years.

In December of 1982, Frank went back to presiding over a courtroom. Within three months, the new chief assigned him a murder case in Grundy County, the first one in 30 years. This trial would change the course of our lives.

**"The court cannot contemplate the execution
of a man without horror."**
– Judge Frank X. Yackley

6 - Murder Trial

The gray three-story courthouse sat in the middle of the town square of Morris, Illinois. Usually cool and quiet, it was buzzing with activity on a July day in 1983, forcing the air conditioning system to work at maximum capacity. The largest of the courtrooms was stuffy and filled with observers including the county elite dressed to the nines, as well as farmers wearing overalls. Spectators spilled into the hallways, adding to the din. Reporters interviewed lawyers in their pinstripe suits, and uniformed sheriff's deputies monitored the scene.

The bailiffs and clerks were busy preparing for the judge's appearance in the final phase of a long and tedious murder trial, the first one in the county in 30 years.

Frank had been assigned the case, and the sentencing process had become a torment. I wanted to be in the courtroom to show my support and admiration. I arrived wearing a silk dress my mother had sewn for me, holding the hand of our teenage son John.

Frank was a compassionate judge, a careful listener who did not prejudge cases, a man with a lot of understanding of the human condition. He applied the law as it was intended and rendered judgments without rancor. He never played to the media. He was also a dedicated champion of civil rights. His decision was of major interest to those for and against the death penalty. Frank had written extensively on the death penalty. In 1977, while serving as state's attorney of LaSalle County, he had testified before the Illinois House Judiciary Committee against capital punishment.

"Frank was the only sitting state's attorney who 'risked' testifying against the death penalty that year," recalled Peg Breslin, who was a representative in the state capital at the time. "That's why his decision on this murder case was of interest to so many."

Frank testified before the Illinois General Assembly that a society should aim to rehabilitate those who are found guilty of a crime however heinous it may be. He believed that sentencing a person to death was not only inhumane, but also reflected poorly on the society that invokes it. He acknowledged that a jury's rendering of a guilty verdict is a grave one and, as such, the punishment should be severe. But he urged lawmakers to spare jurors the option of what he considered an extreme measure.

Despite his passionate arguments, Illinois lawmakers voted to reinstate the death penalty during the summer of 1977.

Six years later, Frank sat quietly in his chambers studying his notes one last time. He had to announce the sentence forced upon him by Illinois law. It was a decision he did not want to make.

His face was pale and drawn when he entered the courtroom. His black robe seemed to weigh heavily on his shoulders. He was exhausted from two months of research, having read hundreds of cases relating to murder sentencing and talked to lawyers, prosecutors, defense attorneys, and appellate judges. He had been looking for a legal loophole to spare a man's life.

When assigned the murder trial, The People vs. John Whitehead, in early 1983, Frank knew he would be facing one of the biggest challenges of his career. Charles Zalar, the state's attorney of Grundy County, and Tony Ficarelli, the assistant attorney general of Illinois, represented the People. Wayne McFarland, public defender, and his assistant, John Hanson, of Grundy County were the defense lawyers. Normally sedate people, they became confrontational and argumentative, often ignoring Frank's gavel and his repeated calls for order in the courtroom.

The mother of Vicki Wrobel, the 5-year-old murder victim who had been kidnapped, raped, strangled, and drowned the previous summer, sat in the first row sobbing day after day. She listened intensely and cringed when the attorneys raised their voices. She seldom spoke as if she were reluctant to do so because of her thick Slovak accent.

The court learned of other crimes committed by the 35-year-old Whitehead who admitted he had raped other young girls, always holding a knife to their throats. He served prison sentences for burglary, assault, and violating parole. Upon his release, he set fire to a woman's trailer home. He also confessed to burglarizing and setting fire to a motel in Wilmington, Illinois, in the middle of the night when all seven rooms were occupied.

Toward the end of May, the jury delivered a guilty verdict of murder and aggravated kidnapping after eight hours of deliberations. Tired and weary, the jurors had one more thing to do: listen to instructions by the judge and agree on a penalty.

For Frank, the worst was yet to come in this long but arduous trial, and it was a shock to everyone in the courtroom. The defense exercised the seldom-used tactic of asking the court to "dismiss the jury and let the judge pass the sentence."

Frank was haunted by those words for the next two months. I read the anguish in his poetry, a hobby he had not indulged in since his college days. I noticed his distress when he got home from work. I felt his tossing and turning in restless sleep at night.

He coiled with disdain when he recalled a reporting assignment at UPI in Chicago in the mid-1960s. He was asked to go to Statesville, the maximum-security prison in Joliet, to witness an execution and write about it. An ambitious reporter who relished tough assignments, he nevertheless refused to cover this story to the chagrin of his editor. "Seeing a helpless man strapped to a chair and electrocuted is against everything I believe in," he told his boss.

Frank's torment deepened as he contemplated the fate of this cold-blooded murderer. He lost weight. He slept very little. He wrote gloomy poetry reflecting his preoccupation with the sentencing task ahead.

Inmate

My Daddy came from Tennessee
To work the shipyards and the docks
In Illinois in 1943
And I was born that year.

They sent him to the penal farm
For burglary in 1949
And sent me here for theft
And statutory rape in 1968.
The guards and inmates beat me bad
In that first week.
But now I work the dogs
And track the prisoners through hickory woods.

My cellmate John Door escaped
And walked 200 miles along the tracks.
The bulls were waiting at his home

And brought him back.
He'd seen the movie "Cool Hand Luke"
And smiled and crinkled up his eyes
And said he didn't give a damn.

My father went to Statesville then
And did three years.
He learned to read and write and went to church.

We built a cell house in the fall.
I laid the mortar and the bricks.
The dogs were with me then.

I'd like to walk the tracks like Johnny did,
And run the woods and keep the fields by night.
My Daddy is a Baptist now,
And writes to me of Saving Grace.

My soul is in the Hickory Woods
Along the tracks on summer nights.

Oh, Jesus Christ, to hell with everyone,
The guards, the inmates and the rest.
I only love the dogs and my old man.
I love the woods
And eating of the honeycomb at night.

Usually a tolerant and non-judgmental person, Frank became impatient and volatile. He was preoccupied and non-communicative. I attributed his behavior to the stress of his job, although his disinterest in our sex life was upsetting. Frank, who once got aroused at the drop of a shoulder strap, began going to bed early and would be asleep by the time I got there. In the morning he would get up quietly before I awakened. He lost interest in the children's activities, once a point of pride for him. Sensing his need for closeness, I decided against taking the children to Turkey that summer. He needed their cheerful company and my presence. I even went ahead with plans to paint the walls downstairs, thinking a little distraction would take Frank's mind off the trial.

My worries about his mental state were reinforced by his overreaction one weekend to a simple request. To prepare the family room to be painted, I put about 80 books into several boxes and asked him to take them to the basement.

"Are you out of your mind, woman?" he yelled. "You are asking me to do mundane chores when I am preparing to go to the moon. You can come along if you want, but don't ask me to move some fucking boxes. Don't you realize that one day I will be a justice in the U.S. Supreme Court? What are you thinking?"

I was shocked by this outburst. Being ambitious was one thing, but this bordered on delusions of grandeur. He was becoming more unpredictable and withdrawing further. Gone were the days he played basketball at the YMCA during his lunch hour; he now preferred to shoot baskets in our backyard. No more corn boils on Congress Street or meetings with his Samuel Johnson Society buddies.

At times he was hyper, other times listless. He became more compulsive, devouring a pound of Brach's Candy in one sitting. He chose the same table at the same restaurant every morning and ordered the same breakfast. He ran at least five miles every morning for 13 months without a break. He would buy three pairs of the same trousers – same style, same color – and get angry when questioned about his choices.

Frank had a beautifully shaped head, big brown eyes, and a bright smile that completed his handsome looks. He started losing his hair at age 19, but had never acted self-conscious about his baldness in all the years I knew him. His father and two older brothers were also bald. In what I later learned, was a manic period, he decided to have a hair transplant and consulted a dermatologist in Oak Brook, Illinois, who described the procedure. First she would make an incision on the top of his head and pull up loose skin to shrink the size of the bald spot. A few months later she would start implanting plugs taken from the back of his head.

I advised against it. "You are in your 40s, having lived with baldness for nearly 25 years. You are healthy, good looking, charming, and loved by your children and me. Why would you put yourself through all this?"

He snapped, "You are my wife, but you don't even know me! You don't know how desperately I want to have hair."

He asked me to accompany him on his next appointment as he sought my assurance that this was a good idea. It was obvious he was not himself. I was convinced I knew him better than he knew himself and that he would not be satisfied with the final outcome.

Not able to dissuade him from the procedure, I volunteered to drive him to the surgery. He turned down my offer, upset by my refusal to endorse his decision. The outpatient procedure with local anesthetic must have taken over an hour. He returned home that evening with his head swathed in bandages. He spent the next three days in a darkened room, moaning about the pain. Eventually, the scar healed into a three-inch perfect line, starting at his crown and reaching the back hairline. If it had not been such a perfect line, one would think it was a wrinkle. He worried it looked like he had a lobotomy. He was obsessed with it, especially since it was so perfect.

"You are tall. Few people can see the scar on the top of your head," I said trying to make him feel better. "What difference does it make? Once you start the transplant process, the scar will be covered up anyway."

He was losing his sense of reason and balance and baffling me by denying that anything was wrong. I began to think he was going through a mid-life crisis and tried to comfort him as he continued to torment himself. He never stopped lamenting about "the fucking scar."

While he was still suffering from this scar, he began to look into corrective eye surgery. Nearsighted since college days, he had been wearing contact lenses for a dozen years. In his 40s, he now complained about dry eyes and said he disliked wearing glasses. So he decided to have corrective eye surgery. This was the early 1980s, and few people had heard of radioscopy. There were one or two ophthalmologists doing the procedure in Illinois, and Frank found a Russian-trained doctor in Winnetka who was willing to operate on his eyes. The surgery was set for late August.

He also bought a motorcycle and a heavy contraption for the back of his Ford LTD to transport it. His shopping sprees for clothes resulted in more arguments, and finally he admitted he was behaving out of character. I wanted to comfort him by pointing out the bright side. "I'd rather you have a hair transplant and ride a motorcycle than acquire a girlfriend," I joked with him.

All summer Frank spent his evenings reading case law, trying to make the "right" decision about John Whitehead's punishment. Once he reached his conclusion, his hyperactivity gave way to quiet reflection and withdrawal. He spent the next few weeks writing and rewriting the sentencing statement he would deliver before a standing-room only crowd.

On that July morning, he was somber as he walked into the courtroom and sat down. He probed the crowd with intense eyes and saw our 13-year-old son standing next to me.

"In a few moments, I am going to announce the sentence in this case and give the reasons for my decision. Of course, it is important that the proceedings continue to be conducted with dignity."

With this bit of caution he slowly, deliberately, and compassionately reviewed the case.

"The court has heard the evidence which resulted in a jury verdict of guilty of murder and aggravated kidnapping. Also, the court has heard evidence and arguments on the death penalty and has taken the matter under advisement. Before pronouncing the sentence, let me make the following findings of fact and conclusions of law.

"Probably the most important aggravating factors in deciding the defendant's punishment are the crimes themselves. The victim was kidnapped, indecent liberties were performed upon her. She was stripped of her clothes and – sometime around midnight on August 9, 1982 – led into the waters of the Mazon River. There the defendant wound his shirt around her neck, twisted it into a ligature, pulled it upwards to choke Vicki Wrobel while he held her under the water until she strangled and drowned."

Frank continued, "Also important as an aggravating factor is the defendant's history and character. From an early age, he has sexually attacked young girls. He has sexually abused his younger sisters, according to records introduced as evidence … and one younger sister testified to eight years of sexual attacks, beatings, and death threats by the defendant."

By his own admission, Whitehead had sexually abused other young girls, often while assaulting them with a knife, Frank pointed out. Many of the attacks occurred while the defendant was a juvenile and continued into his adult life.

"The list of his crimes is countless because – by his own words which appear in this record – he sought his young victims along railroad tracks, lonely parks, and other remote places where he could carry out his sexual attacks while wielding a knife to frighten the little girls so they would not reveal what happened," Frank read from the statement.

A pattern of repeated lies by the defendant defeated the argument that he did not remember the murder and that he had suffered a blackout during the hours when Vicki was kidnapped and killed, Frank explained.

"Shortly after the murder, the defendant confessed several times in great detail, revealing facts known only to a person who was present when Vicki was killed. He lied under oath when it suited him; spoke of fevers that compelled him to commit sex crimes, fevers that took a week to develop before they culminated in a violent act. With all this extra warning time, why didn't he seek help?"

Frank cleared his throat and read from his carefully prepared text.

"The court finds there is little evidence in mitigation. The defendant relies on brainwave tests and the testimony of Dr. Ziporyn to support a theory of mental illness. The evidence of such illness is very slight and not credible. Dr. Hughes, who conducted the brainwave tests, said that according to experts, 24 percent of normal persons have brainwave characteristics similar to the defendant's. The court finds that the brainwave evidence is insignificant."

He added that during the defendant's hospitalization in 1975, eight years before Vicki's murder, doctors found no evidence of psychosis and no evidence of mental illness. A similar opinion by another doctor was rendered before the trial. That year, a clinical psychologist found the defendant to be "astute, shrewd, calculating, and bright." The doctor found him to be "cagey, purposely evasive and avoiding, and seemingly insincere." That examination came after his arrest on a charge of rape. In that trial, he first testified he had amnesia, then changed his story to consensual sex at which time he was found not guilty.

Frank acknowledged that Whitehead was brutally mistreated by his father when he was a child. "While this might go some distance in explaining the defendant's own abuse of children, in no way does it excuse or justify such abuse. John Whitehead had the intelligence to seek help and treatment, but chose instead to give in to his grotesque urges. When he killed Vicki Wrobel, he acted with characteristic shrewdness and calculation. He watched the child in a playground, surrounded by cars with keys in the ignition, a common practice in close-knit rural communities. Whitehead snatched the key to one car and, when that was discovered, returned it and snatched the key to another car. He watched and waited until the child was alone. Then he picked her up and drove 31 miles to a remote location with which he was familiar."

Frank ruled that the defendant was not under the influence of any extreme mental or emotional distress when he killed Vicki. To make sure he covered all the bases he quoted from letters written on behalf of the defendant – letters from his mother, sister, and a friend he met in the Union County Jail.

"The court is moved to pity by these letters and cannot contemplate the execution of a man without horror. The very thought of taking the condemned man from his cell in the night hours, leading him down a passageway to the death chamber where he is placed in the deadly apparatus and deliberately killed – the whole procedure is impossible to contemplate without horror and dread. And yet based on all the evidence, particularly on the cruelty of Vicki Wrobel's murder, as well as the many crimes of the defendant, especially his sex crimes, his knife assaults, and his crimes of arson, the court is impelled toward the conclusion that the proper sentence for John Whitehead is death. Therefore, the court, concluding that no other sentence would be proper, hereby sentences John Whitehead to death for the murder of Vicki Wrobel."

Frank ignored the stir of excitement in the courtroom to announce another sentence on Whitehead: an additional 30 years in prison for aggravated kidnapping. Illinois law requires separate and additional sentencing for a guilty verdict of aggravated kidnapping.

With dignity and compassion, Frank explained why he had gone against his principles and sentenced a man to death.

"All my life I have been against taking a man's life, regardless of his guilt," he said. "But as a judge and an agent of the state, I have to follow the law. The law directs me to the sentence of death."

Reporters scurried out to meet deadlines as attorneys and fellow judges whispered approval of Frank's performance. Trial spectators went their separate ways left to discuss the outcome of the first murder trial in Grundy County in three decades.

"Finally," I thought, "this ordeal is over. We will get back to normal."

But it would soon become clear Frank had passed a death sentence on himself as well as on John Whitehead.

> **"Manic depression is a frustrating mess**
> **Well, I think I'll go turn myself off,**
> **And go on down, all the way down."**
> – Jimi Hendrix

7 - Chemical Imbalance

Despite the fact he was a poor traveler, Frank agreed to spend a week at a tennis camp in central Michigan after the sentencing. The goal was to improve our performance against the three couples with whom we played doubles. Our children were at a YMCA summer camp in Michigan, and we decided Frank needed to get away to enjoy physical activity and sunshine. I hoped this diversion would ease the stress brought on by the trial and sentencing.

My intentions were stymied, and he was soon in a deeper depression, as though he could not escape the demons overtaking his life. It was obvious from the beginning that he had no energy for tennis. He was unable to concentrate on his form or focus on the game. He was unwilling to correct his serves or change his backhand as suggested by the college-age tennis pros who good-naturedly teased him about his game. He was so self-conscious about the bandage hiding the scar on the top of his head that he wore a baseball cap on and off the tennis courts. Never much at making small talk, he was seen as unfriendly by players on the courts and diners in the cafeteria.

An older couple from Waco, Texas befriended us. The wife, a psychologist, noted Frank's depression and was unsuccessful in her attempt to bring him out of his despair. Privately, she told me that Frank should see a doctor. After what seemed like the longest week of my life, I drove home holding back tears.

I had suggested for months that he talk to a professional, and I continued my campaign even more vigorously upon our return. I reminded him that at the sentencing hearing he had found fault with John Whitehead who had the intelligence to seek help but did not do so.

"Don't compare me with a murderer. There is nothing wrong with me. I am just exhausted from the trial and upset about the fucking scar on my head. I will be okay," was his typical answer.

I was surprised and happy when, in the middle of August, he called the eye doctor in Winnetka to cancel the corrective surgery. He finally realized he could not handle one more radical procedure. He also informed me that he had decided against the hair transplant.

Our children returned from camp suntanned and happy, ready to share their adventures with their dad. But he was uninterested, marooned in his despondency. As the new school year began, I prayed for the return to our routine, uneventful life.

That Labor Day was warm and humid. The children were playing outside, and I assumed Frank was in the basement engaged in one of his favorite hobbies, matting and framing historic photographs or lifting weights. During better days, he had turned half the basement into a workshop and the other half into a gym. Therein he stored hundreds of frames he bought at art shops or garage sales and stacked various pieces of glass to fit the frames. His matte cutter, staple gun, colorful boards, glue, and special felt pens were lined up at one end of the workbench and his stereo at the other. He would play classical music or listen to Irish tenors and say to me, "I am preparing for my old age. You want a husband with hobbies so he does not drive you crazy when he retires, right?" He enjoyed matting action shots of sports heroes for the boys and Degas ballerinas for Ayla's room. The gym consisted of several benches with bars and heavy weights, pull-up stations, a rowing machine, a punching bag, and dumbbells.

That afternoon there was no sign of Frank in the basement, the kitchen, or the family room. The house was quiet. Maybe he's taking a nap, I thought. Tiptoeing up to our bedroom, which was darkened by drawn shades, I discovered him curled up in a fetus position, shaking and sobbing.

"Honey, what's wrong? Why are you so sad?" I asked.

"I don't know. I don't know. I feel so depressed." I put my arms around him as he whispered, "If I had a gun, I'd kill myself."

My heart stopped for a second, and I knew I must act quickly. Even though he did not want anyone to know how hopeless he felt, I called Dr. German Gonzalo, a good friend and Joe's godfather, who quickly made arrangements for Frank to see a new psychiatrist in town.

As we left to meet the doctor, I was in such a daze that I barely said goodbye to the boys. Ayla was across town visiting a friend. Frank was unusually compliant as I led him to the passenger side of our station wagon still in the garage. A friend's dog was fussing about the car but his owners called for him and he ran out. I began backing up and immediately felt the back tire on my side of the car hit something, and I heard a squealing meow.

I got out of the car and bent down to look under the tire to find the lifeless body of Pony, Ayla's little kitten. Apparently, Pony had sought refuge from the dog under our car and, startled as the engine turned over, tried to get away. Knowing I had to get Frank to the hospital where the doctor was waiting, I scooped up Pony's limp body and put it in a plastic bag to be buried in the back yard upon our return.

Within minutes after arriving at the emergency room, we were talking to Dr. Joseph Chuprevich, a hospital psychiatrist, about Frank's desperation, his family background, his stress on the job, weight loss, sleepless nights, and his overreaction to everyday occurrences. It took the doctor less than an hour to diagnose Frank's condition as manic depression.

"What caused this, how did it happen?" we asked.

Frank, at age 46, was at the top of his judicial career. Those who knew him thought he was brilliant, friendly, and charming. He kept himself in excellent physical condition by running and lifting weights every day. He ate well-balanced meals, took his vitamins, and got plenty of sleep. He was a devoted father who preferred shooting baskets with the neighborhood kids to drinking beer with his buddies. He was loved by friends and respected by foes. Married for 17 years and parents of three bright and healthy children, we lived in a three-story brick home on a tree-lined street in an affluent neighborhood.

The doctor explained that a crisis or extreme stress often brings on a nervous breakdown. "From what you've told me, there is an apparent tendency toward depression in your family, and often it lays dormant until something triggers it," he addressed Frank. "In your case, the murder trial and the torment you went through before sentencing may have resulted in your illness." He prescribed antidepressants, made an appointment to see us again in two weeks, and sent us home.

We learned that bipolar illness, or manic-depressive disorder, is an ancient disease with descriptions appearing in the Biblical Old Testament and in writings from classical Greece. Despite centuries of recognition, manic depression is one of the least studied of all mental illnesses and it remains an enigmatic and often destructive condition. It embodies the meaning of the word "opposite." It is differentiated from other forms of depression by its periods of intense mania or hypo-mania. Sufferers experience black and hopeless moods of depression as well as euphoric feelings of mania.

Once we returned from seeing the doctor we told Ayla her kitten had been killed. She seemed more frightened by tears. I was crying not only for Pony but about what faced our family. Frank dug a hole in the backyard, and we buried Pony. A few weeks later, Ayla and I went to the veterinarian's office and adopted a homeless cat Frank named Rookie.

But he was mostly like a robot during the next few weeks. He would go to work, come home, and then follow me around like a child.

"Please, please don't leave me," he mumbled. "Don't let me go back to 310 Spring Street," the address of his family home in Naperville where his unmarried sister and brother lived.

For the first time Frank confided that in 1954 an admissions counselor at DePaul University in Chicago told him to see a psychologist after reviewing his aptitude test. The counselor, acknowledging that Frank had a high I.Q., must have been alarmed about something in his test results.

"Who went to psychologists in the 1950s?" Frank said, but always wondered why the counselor had made such a recommendation.

I was afraid Frank's psyche had crossed the line from brilliance to madness. What I assumed was ambition, adventure, and brightness now seemed like mood swings, indecisiveness, and impulsive behavior.

I wondered why he had waited twenty-five years to tell me about the counselor's comments. Perhaps he feared knowing this fact would have kept me from marrying him. After all, he had told me about his relatives who suffered mental illness. Had I ignored the potential implications?

Desperate about his state of mind, Frank considered giving up his judgeship even though the doctor assured him his condition would not affect his job performance. He did not need hospitalization. "Give the antidepressants time to work," we were told.

Nevertheless, Frank was devastated, angry, and in total denial. "Can you believe it? The doctor says I am fucking crazy. No way am I crazy. No way!"

We read whatever books we could find about manic depression, and I learned this was like other chronic illnesses, such as diabetes, epilepsy, or heart disease. "Just take your medication and see the doctor every two weeks. We're lucky you're not terminally ill," I told him.

Secrets are hard to keep in a small community, and the problems of prominent residents could become the talk of the town. Frank was more concerned about what people would think than how we could cope with his illness. He hated the prospect of being on medication for the rest of his life and rejected the idea that he was suffering from a chemical imbalance. Frank had a lifelong dislike for doctors and taking medication.

The psychiatrist asked me to keep track of Frank's mood swings on a calendar. Frequent changes signaled a more serious bipolar illness. For a month or so, he would be hyper, gregarious, funny, and sleepless. Then suddenly he would sink into the depths of despair, lying around the house, morose, and sleeping 10 hours a day. He was self- absorbed and upset with us for being cheerful. "You don't know how hopeless and dark life seems," he told me. "You have never been depressed, so you cannot understand."

Out of love and respect, we tiptoed around the house, never realizing we were subconsciously matching his moods.

He continued running, sometimes 10 or 15 miles a day. One day on his return from one of these long runs he wrote this poem, which I overheard him read to the children. It made me cringe.

Rat *(with apologies to Bobby Burns)*

I saw you lying on the road and
didn't know at first you were dead
but then I saw the flies –
a car or truck had shut the light
within your tiny brain.

I see you're fat and had your fill
within these fields of corn and beans
and laughed to see the farmers work
to feed your kids.
To hell with the farmers in this town,
and all the cars and trucks.
You had your fun,
you ate and ate the corn
on summer nights
and never worked a day.

And winter's coming anyway
and there is work in eating then, and cold.

So lie there on the road
and let the cars run up and down.
You lived and laughed at farmers in the fields
and you go to where there's neither corn nor beans,
just endless nights in heaven or in hell
for stealing in these farms.
Good night, old friend.
We'll never meet again
around these fields.
You'll never run again on summer nights
Or laugh to see the farmers at their work.

It took about six weeks for new medication to work and for Frank to feel better. Some normalcy returned to our daily lives, and he was almost his old self, telling funny stories about his childhood and laughing until he cried. His sharp sense of humor and capacity to recall anecdotes mesmerized me and the children.

He was quick to praise our kids when they accomplished something and was there to comfort them when they were upset.

His love, pride, and wit come across in this poem written after one of John's high school cross-country races:

Miler *(to John)*

You won my heart by gliding in the sun
on summer days.
Your smooth, white legs were floating in the sun
and never touched the ground.
Like Icarus, you flew.
'You never train,' said Paul, your friend.
'I train,' you said,
'by wrestling at the movies with the girls.'
You never showed the strain
except the last 100 yards,
when pain was written in your heart
and on your handsome face.
I loved you best the day you won the race
by 40 yards
in borrowed shoes
and only trained
by wrestling lightly at the drive-in with the girls.

One late spring afternoon Ayla's love for animals and her desire to walk the neighbor's dog nearly ended in tragedy. She had taken Buckers by the bluff overlooking the Fox River near our home. We think Buckers got curious and agitated about the scent of a raccoon or squirrel and pulled at his leash. What looked like solid ground to Ayla turned out to be discarded leaves, and with one wrong step she and Buckers slipped and slid into the cold water of the river.

The current is fast at the river's bend where the Fox flows into the Illinois River. Ayla, a strong swimmer, stayed calm, even at 12-years-old, and held Buckers up while treading water. Two boaters near the opposite shore spotted her, motored over, and pulled them out of the water. I still shudder when I think about this near-tragedy and remember my shock at seeing my soaking-wet and shivering daughter brought home by a policeman.

Once again Frank expressed his emotions in a poem:

Fall

I think of cats and dogs,
of a dog named Turtle and a cat called Pony.
I love the dog Turtle
and the cat called Pony
and I love the dog Buckers
and he loves me.

I tumbled down the rocks
with the dog named Buckers
and God heard me scream.

I sank in the water
and I went down.

The seaweed twisted in my hair
and sand poured in my shoes.

I saw God's face under the waves
and the Lord reached down and pulled me up
and I saved Buckers and God saved me.
I love the dog Turtle and the cat called Pony
And I love the dog Buckers and he loves me.

These freak accidents, rebellious behavior by the children, and my husband's frantic frame of mind began to take a toll on me. The balancing act of keeping an eye on Frank, meeting the children's emotional needs, and running a household made me jittery. I usually fell into bed totally exhausted. One such night a loud crash awakened us from deep sleep around 2 a.m. We ran to the back of the house from where the noise had come. Noticing John was not in his bed and the porch door that led down the backstairs to the driveway was wide open, I quickly switched on the flood light and saw Frank's 1976 Ford LTD wedged against a corner of the garage.

John, not yet 15 and without the benefit of driver's education classes, had decided he would take his dad's car on a joyride. Instead he had pinned himself in the old and narrow garage. It took Frank and a neighbor the whole day to jack up the car, loosen and lift it to its original position. Repairs to the car and the garage took several days. I grounded John for a month despite Frank's objections that I was being too harsh.

Even after admitting that Ayla was high-strung, Frank insisted I should not be hard on her either. "Do not break her spirit," he admonished when I complained about her defiant and uncooperative behavior. She continually disregarded the rules and tested my patience over and over again. Getting her up in the mornings was a major struggle. Junior high was four miles across town, and because Frank was usually gone by the time Ayla was ready for school, I would have to drive her to school when she overslept.

"If you get up late and miss the bus one more time, you will ride your bike or walk to school," I said. "And I don't care if you are late to class."

One weekday morning in the fall, after Frank had left for work, John walked the two blocks to the high school, Joe took his bus to grade school, and Ayla was still upstairs as the bus pulled away. "Start biking," I called to her. Suddenly, hearing a thud, I ran upstairs to find her trying to climb out of the second-floor window by way of sheets tied together like a rope. It was a rather elaborate effort to run away.

I called the school psychologist who explained that Ayla was sensing the undercurrents in the household. "How is your marriage?" he asked. Before I could deny anything was wrong, he said, "Ayla's antennae are picking up signals that you probably don't even realize you are broadcasting."

I was frustrated and short-tempered. Too often I picked on the children, especially Ayla, who butted heads with me. Her feistiness further taxed my patience. I decided I needed professional help and enrolled in a parenting class offered by St. Columba Church. I kept a diary and wrote down all sorts of sensible options, such as counting to 10 before screaming, taking deep, long breaths, diverting her attention, or quietly leaving the room.

Despite the effort, Ayla continued to get under my skin. One day she arrived home in a lousy mood demanding something. As soon as I told her no, she threw a tantrum. As I had been taught in the parenting class, I tried to put my arms around her to calm her down, but she started pulling my hair with all her might. I lost my cool and pulled her hair back. There we were screaming in pain and acting like two alley cats. When I finally pulled away, I called Frank at work to "do something about your daughter."

I became the loser in this episode because Frank was furious with me for bothering him at work, and Ayla was satisfied she had received a lot of attention. Ayla's strong will and domineering personality irritated her brothers, also. Interaction among family members often spun out of control. Still, Frank and I tried to do certain normal things as a family, such as winter outings at Chestnut Mountain, a ski resort near Galena, Illinois. December 1984 was a snowy month so we looked forward to a great getaway. Country roads are treacherous when there is blowing snow, and on this drive the roads were icy too.

Normally a cautious driver, Frank was exuberant and hyperactive that day. He chatted non-stop, telling jokes, and going too fast in these conditions. An hour into our trip, the station wagon hit a patch of ice and spun out of control, made a 360-degree turn, and got stuck in a snow bank. We were pretty shook up, but not hurt. It took an hour to get the car back on the road, and Frank was now in a foul mood.

As we ate lunch at a truck stop nearby, Frank went to the pay phone and cancelled our reservation at Chestnut Mountain. Arguing with him would only make matters worse, and, anyway, I did not feel like spending three days with a sulking husband.

After incidents like these, I was suspicious that Frank was not taking his medication regularly. Without being a nag, I would try to encourage him not to fool with the dosage. Sometimes he'd admit that he was trying to wean himself off the pills, other times he'd tell me he knew what he was doing. "I have to lick this thing. I will find a way out."

During spring break in 1985, I was asked to attend a school board convention in Anaheim, California, having served nine years on the Ottawa Elementary School Board. Families were welcome so long as they paid their way. Frank decided he and the children would come along. They planned to go to Disneyland and Knotts' Berry Farm while I was in conferences, and we could have nice, leisurely dinners together.

All went well initially.   The children were old enough to lounge around the motel and the swimming pool.   Eventually Frank, wanting time alone, took our rental car and went shopping in Laguna Beach. He bought three huge barrel-like ceramic pots without figuring out how he was going to get them home to Ottawa. He said he had a great day, but was tired and wanted to go to bed shortly after dinner.

The kids wanted to go to a movie. Although I was tired too, I started to drive them to a mall but soon ran out of patience with their quarreling on the way back to the hotel. When they ignored my orders for quiet, I lost my cool and told them they would have to walk to the hotel if they did not stop misbehaving. They ignored me, and I promptly pulled over and ordered them out of the car.

I got back to the hotel and saw that Frank was ready to put down his book and go to sleep, but we waited up for the children. They marched in an hour or so later, furious with me, and refused to be quiet. Though we had a large room, it was overcrowded with five of us.   Between John's anger, Ayla's whining, and Joe's complaints, a fuse blew in Frank's head, and he started shouting and cursing at all of us. Joe and Ayla cowered in the bathroom. I pleaded with him to calm down and reminded him the walls were thin, that we were disturbing other guests. That made him scream even louder. Soon there was a knock on the door from security guards investigating the noise. The next day Frank told us he would be changing his ticket and flying home a day earlier. This incident was so upsetting to me that I was glad to see him go.

In those days the closest center for bipolar disorders was Rush Presbyterian Hospital in Chicago, 80 miles away.   I tried to persuade Frank to seek the help of specialists or find a support group. He reminded me he had been seeing a psychiatrist since September 1983. "I am satisfied with him," he said. "Why would I want to drive to Chicago? We cannot broadcast my troubles to the whole world." Frank left little room for negotiation in those days. I found it easier to drop the subject.

I became more and more frustrated and lonely, and I longed for my mother. She knew Frank was depressed and suggested I bring him to Turkey. She reminded me how he had enjoyed our trip in 1975 when she had engineered an invitation for Frank, then state's attorney, to speak to the Ankara and Istanbul Bar Associations about the jury system in the United States. Turkey's criminal code is based on the Italian penal system where a judge or a panel of judges rules on the guilt or innocence of a defendant. We had paid our own way, but Frank was delighted to be wined and dined by his colleagues across the ocean.

"He needs a change. Bring him to Erdek," she said insisting he would feel better if he spent a few weeks by the sea. I wanted to tell her, face-to-face, how much more serious Frank's illness was. I needed her sympathy, her advice, her hugs, to chase away the dark clouds. She and my father had always been there for me, arriving from Turkey for the birth of both boys and staying to help care for them. They also took the children under their wings during summers. They were wonderful parents and grandparents.

> **"A little madness in the Spring**
> **Is wholesome even for the King."**
> – Emily Dickinson

8 - Outside Interference

In denial about his illness, Frank did not want to follow his doctor's orders, nor listen to my pleas to get a second opinion. He disliked being on medication, and as soon as he began feeling like he could cope, he would reduce the dosage and soon enter a manic phase.

"I don't want to be mellow and listless. I like feeling high," he said, knowing that the medicine would bring him down from his euphoria.

I was fearful that Frank's life was spiraling out of control during the three years following the murder trial. His behavior ranged from impulsive to bizarre. He bragged about running 378 straight days without a break and through all four seasons. He went on shopping sprees, rode around on his motorcycle at odd times, obsessed about his baldness and poor eyesight, and spent more and more time away from home. He gave up going to church and pulled away from friends and family. He was acting so much out of character that I began to wonder what kind of man I had married.

Still, I devoted my energies to keeping normalcy-, both at home and outside the home. When Frank was depressed and did not want to accept an invitation to speak or attend a social function, I went in his place or made up an excuse for him. Like the wife of an alcoholic, I was becoming an enabler –covering up his inadequacies, making excuses for him, and giving him cause to pull further into his cocoon. When he was manic, I listened patiently to his grandiose ideas. As Frank's values, goals, ambitions, and hopes for himself and for our children grew hazy, my load became heavier. I was frustrated and confused with nowhere to go.

Our family kept Frank's illness secret. Only the children and Frank's siblings knew he was bipolar. It was a struggle to maintain the impression everything in our lives was normal. His psychiatrist urged him to share his torment with a close friend, like fellow judge Bob Carter who would understand.

"No, I don't want anyone to know," he said. He felt ashamed.

I felt lonely since Frank was not communicating with me and I could not talk about our situation with anyone in town. Frank's sister-in-law Betty, the psychologist, was willing to help, but she lived 50 miles away. She was a comfort to me, listening to my frustrations and sharing the Yackley family's mental health secrets. But her attempts to counsel Frank backfired. He did not like her direct, self-help approach. Having known him since he was 13, her advice was simple:

"You are a smart fellow and responsible for your own happiness. Pull yourself up by your boot straps."

A few years back, with Frank's encouragement and support, I had opened a public relations agency Say It With Sel, handling retail advertising for local merchants, writing and editing newsletters for organizations, and doing press releases for businesses.   One of my clients was Peg Breslin, our state representative.   Every two years I would help her raise funds, manage her political campaign, and enlist volunteers to get out the vote.   One volunteer, Susan Post, made a positive impression on me.   Though she had not gone to college, she was capable and well-informed.   When Peg's legislative aide retired, I recommended Susan take her place.   Over the next four years, we worked well together and became friends.

On election day in 1984 I was to meet Frank at the local coffee shop for breakfast.   By 7 a.m., I found myself so busy assigning poll watchers, checking on election judges, and arranging for drivers that I sent Susan to have breakfast with Frank, even though they hardly knew each other.

I was happy to see that for the next several months their friendship grew.   They often had a cup of coffee together or she visited him in his chambers to discuss constituent problems.   She also came to our home frequently, sometimes bearing gifts for the children.   Often she ended up in the basement talking to Frank while he pursued one of his hobbies.   I encouraged these visits, thinking at least Frank was not isolating himself completely.   I had no fear that their relationship was anything more than friendship because Susan was a good Catholic, married with two teen-age children, and my friend.

Our family was used to Frank going to his office on Sundays to catch up with paperwork, but he would stay close to home most weeknights.   Then he began to go a couple of evenings a week.   On several occasions, I could not reach him in his chambers with urgent messages from sheriff's deputies or fellow judges.   When confronted, he would say, "I was doing research in the library," or "I was making copies in the copy center."

Never suspicious, I accepted his explanations.   He had been a faithful husband for 18 years.   Lately, he had been paying little attention to me, and our sex life was nonexistent, but the doctor had said antidepressants would reduce his sex drive. So I never complained or brought up the subject.

During the next year, I continued with my public relations work, teaching at the community college, and volunteering for charitable organizations. I became pragmatic and detached as Frank's mood swings became more frequent and as he continued to ignore me. I avoided confrontations, wanting to spare the children additional heartache. I excused, even ignored, his self-absorption.

Growing up with older and tired parents, Frank had pretty much raised himself and could not understand why I wanted a close-knit family and tight supervision of our kids. He enjoyed being a buddy to our boys rather than being their father, relating to them by playing sports or telling jokes, sometimes off-color ones.

"Take it easy on them," he would say when I insisted on knowing where they were going and when they would be back or having them finish their chores for their weekly allowance.

I knew Frank loved the children "more than my own soul," as he wrote in a letter to them shortly before his suicide, and his love and devotion gave them a solid foundation. Before he became ill he spent a lot of time with them, telling stories about his childhood, talking about historic figures, quoting from famous speeches, or reciting poetry. Though he lacked fathering skills such as guidance and disciplining, he was a great role model in physical fitness, honesty, humility, and compassion.

Frank's favorite was Joe, a sweet, easy-going boy with curly blonde hair, big green eyes, and a gentle manner that won everyone's heart. Frank was so attached to him that when Joe turned nine he convinced me to break the family tradition and not send Joe to Germany to live with my sister and her husband. John and Ayla had spent 14 months, respectively, in 1979 and 1981, with Nil and Torhan while attending fourth grade at the Grasdorf Elementary School, becoming multi-cultural and trilingual. It would have been Joe's turn in 1984.

"Being away from him all summer is lonely enough, but I cannot be without him a whole year," Frank said. "I enjoy his company, I like taking him on bike rides and hikes. He needs time alone with me because our older kids are so overbearing and bossy."

Ten years after Frank's death my sister produced a letter from Frank written when Joe turned 11, regretting this decision. He asked her to extend a similar invitation to Joe, which he accepted after he finished college. Joe did graduate work at Hanover University in the late 1990s.

John, a mature and independent young man at age 15, saw life more objectively and put distance between himself and his dad. Every April he delighted in leaving Ottawa High School for Hanover, Germany, where he spent four months at the Gymnasium, a college-prep high school. While living with my sister and her husband, he witnessed a different kind of family life and became aware of his father's shortcomings.

Awed by John's accomplishments, Frank once told me, "I look up to John as a boy would look up to his dad. John is everything I am not: self-confident, smart, a good athlete, and a leader." John was captain of the swim and cross country teams and president of the student council. Frank was overjoyed when John won speech tournaments and touched by his humble acceptance of defeat in backyard basketball or street touch football. He would tell him not to let anyone bully him and laugh at the pranks John would play on the neighbors. He was envious that John was as much at home in Germany and in Turkey as he was in America. He often repeated the story that John, at age 5, returned home from a summer in Turkey and forgot his English. Since Frank knew no Turkish, the two of them used sign language and laughed at the neighbor kids' chanting, "Johnny can't talk. Johnny can't talk."

Ayla, our middle child, was spirited, imaginative, stubborn, and sensitive. By age 11, she would constantly clash with me and expect her dad to intervene on her behalf. Frank, not knowing how to handle a daughter, seemed tentative in the way he interacted with her. She liked visiting his chambers and, in the old days, watching him prosecute drug dealers, tax evaders, or burglars.

As a little girl, she acted out her daydreams, talked to an imaginary friend, and listened to the same story over and over again – her favorite was "The Little Engine That Could." Growing up, she buried herself in books, often inviting friends to our home to read Nancy Drew adventures in the comfort of a cardboard miniature home in our basement.

Touching were the moments when Frank read to the children stories like Stephen Vincent Benet's The Devil and Daniel Webster during road trips as I drove or at home on snowy days. The kids were allowed only one hour of television a night, and Frank would get down on the floor with them stretching out his arms and fashioning them into pillows. Often there would be arguments between the children about who would be right next to him. Two heads ended up on one arm and the third on the other as they watched favorite shows like "Cheers," "Family Ties," or "The Dukes of Hazard." When he worked as a state's attorney, often he would take the children to Berta's, a tavern that served delicious hamburgers. He would drink beer and shoot the breeze with the sheriff's deputies or young attorneys while the children played pool. On school holidays or Saturdays he liked going to breakfast with one of the children in turn. "I like handling one kid at a time because it feels special for both of us," he said. Frank's friends would sit at their table and talk about local politics and sports with the children involved in their conversation.

During the summer of 1985, I took the children to Turkey. Several friends questioned me about my two-month absence from home. "How can you leave your husband for such a long time?" they asked. Frank loved to be alone; he needed his space and refused dinner invitations while we were gone. I told friends that

Frank enjoyed his summers alone, managed well, and would never look at another woman.

Two incidents upon my return that year made me later realize I was wrong to be so trusting.

The first one had to do with my arrival at O'Hare a few weeks ahead of the children. Even though my flight was to arrive late enough for Frank to drive the 80 miles from Ottawa to pick me up, he had arranged for our good friend, 82-year-old Bill Heinz, to do the honors.

Poor judgment, I thought. Bill had a minor accident and never made it to the airport. I called Frank at every number I could think of with no luck. Exhausted from the 15-hour trip, I finally reached a neighbor who met me at the train station in Joliet. When I arrived home Frank was non-communicative, in no mood to answer my questions or accept blame. Once again I was silent, but cursed Frank's bipolar disorder.

The second incident took place a week after the children returned from Turkey. Frank, active with the Illinois Judges Association, often attended meetings in Chicago and asked us to come along for the four-day conference that preceded Labor Day. I always enjoyed going to Chicago with Frank, and the kids were excited about visiting museums, the Lincoln Park Zoo, and swimming at Oak Street Beach.

I noticed Frank was cross and fidgety as we packed our bags and the kids ran in and out of the house making a ruckus. Suddenly, Frank screamed, "Shut up!" Then he said he had changed his mind and was not taking us along. "As a matter of fact, I am not going either," he said. "I am sick and tired of all of you. I want out."

Joe, who was not yet 11, could not figure out what was happening. He put his arms around Frank's neck and started crying. "What did we do, Dad? Why are you leaving us?"

I was shocked, angry, and at a loss for words. I knew Frank was hurting, but why was he hurting us, too? I could understand if he was unhappy in our marriage, but not his rejection of the children. Frank stormed out of the house with suitcase in hand and left me the task of reassuring the children we would be okay. I struggled to hide my true emotions and the sinking feeling that tougher times were ahead.

Frank returned the next evening and apologized for his abrupt behavior. He said he had ditched the meeting in Chicago and stayed at a motel in town. This time I was not going to forgive him for putting us through such torment. I surprised myself with my chutzpah and told him to sleep on the sofa in the family room until "I am ready to invite you back to our bed." He bitched and griped for the next few nights, telling me I was embarrassing him in front of the children and he was not getting enough sleep. Within a week he was back in our bedroom.

Early in October Susan Post confided in Peg and me that she had left her husband.

"I am sick and tired of his smoking, screaming, and aggressive behavior," she said. "It took me months to get the courage to walk out on him after 25 years."

During the next seven months Frank continued to complain about his dissatisfaction with our marriage, his life in Ottawa, and his isolation as a judge. The pattern of wanting to change careers every seven years was repeating itself. He applied for an administrative job in Springfield, the state capital, asking me to type his resume. He also asked me to accompany him on his interview with then-Chief Justice Seymour Simon of the Illinois Supreme Court. The position in Springfield was offered to someone else. Nevertheless, Frank kept telling me he needed a change and that he needed space. Soon he was looking for an apartment to rent. It wasn't a good idea for a bipolar person to remove himself from his source of support, but I rationalized that a few months away from the kids might bring him to his senses. In my naiveté I did not pick up on the subtle hints from friends suggesting that Frank was seeing another woman.

"I trust Frank more than I trust myself," I once told the psychiatrist when he asked if I thought Frank had a girlfriend. It was shortly after this conversation that Dr. Chuprevich told me he could not see the two of us together anymore and that he could recommend a colleague for me to see if I needed to talk to a professional.

On the morning of Good Friday 1986, a month before our 20th wedding anniversary, I returned home from working out at the YMCA. As I put a bouquet of flowers I had purchased for Easter in a vase, I noticed Frank busily packing.

"I am moving out, taking some personal belongings. The movers will come and get the furniture you can spare on Monday," he said.

I was thunderstruck.

"Are you sure you want to do this?" I asked, suggesting he needed the love and support of his family.

"I've been thinking about this for months," he answered. "I found a great apartment overlooking the Illinois River. I am leaving you."

Just like that. So sure of himself, so decisive – so unlike Frank.

With a heavy heart that Monday, I watched the movers pack the bookcases, the sofa bed, the spare dining set, Frank's weight-lifting equipment, and his frames and mats. I was numb that Frank could leave us. After the movers left, I felt the need to talk to someone about my predicament and drove the six blocks to Peg's office. I parked the car in the back alley and used my key to enter. The afternoon sun was fading and the office lights were on. Susan was alone and startled to see me. My face muscles were tense, my lips turned down.

"Remember what a good listener I was when you told me about leaving your husband last fall?" I began. "You were proud of yourself for having left him."

She gave me a strange glance and waited.

"Now, I need someone to listen to me. Frank just moved out," I said, tears welling up in my eyes. The more I talked about how disappointed and horrible I was feeling, the quieter Susan became. I looked up at her and noticed the blood had drained from her face. She interrupted me,

"I am not the right person for you to talk to about this," she said coldly.

"Why not?" I asked.

"Because I think too much of Frank. I love him," she said, nervously tripping over the words.

My heart pounded. My head throbbed. My throat went dry. I froze. I shook my head to regain my composure and looked at Susan. "She must be joking," I prayed, but the look on her face told me she wasn't.

She then smiled oddly and came toward me with open arms for an embrace. I retreated, muttering, "It can't be." I rushed out of the office to my car. I don't remember how I drove home.

Flashbacks came like lightening bolts. I figured the Labor Day weekend episode was a coordinated effort for Susan and Frank to leave their spouses and children at the same time. She had done so, but it took Frank seven months to find the courage to follow suit. The job in Springfield would have given Frank a chance to spend time with Susan away from the watchful eyes of our friends and neighbors. His weeknight absences also made sense.

John was the first person I saw upon my return home.

"I think your dad has been having an affair," I told him.

He shook his head gravely. "Dad just called. He's coming home to pick up the rest of his things," he said.

My hair tousled and eyes red from crying, I confronted Frank as he walked into the kitchen through the backdoor.

"You have to explain to me a lot of things," I said, signaling him to follow me to the quiet of the living room. Without giving him a chance to speak, I bombarded him with questions.

"Susan tells me she loves you. Are you having an affair? Is that why you moved out? Have you slept with her?"

His head hung low as he nodded "yes" to each question.

I held back tears as I shouted, "How could you?"

I was on the offensive. "You have to explain everything to the children. You must tell them the truth."

Frank stood there looking like a spoiled child and called for John to gather Ayla and Joe into the living room. He then walked over to our white couch in front of the picture window overlooking Congress Street and sat down. He was quiet at first, searching for a way to tell them the truth. Sitting in separate armchairs across the room, exuding anxiety, the children fidgeted, pulling at their shoelaces and smoothing their T-shirts and shorts. Tears ran down my cheeks, and sobs escaped my lips as I paced the area between the entryway and the living room, listening to every word that came out of Frank's mouth.

With a trembling voice and a slow but deliberate tone Frank touched upon his relationship with Susan and tried to explain why he was leaving us. It was pitiful and heartbreaking. He talked about his alcoholic and sometimes violent father and about his tired, old mother who never hugged or kissed him. He told them about the Catholic Church that kept him on the straight and narrow and celibate until our marriage. He also claimed that being a judge isolated him from ordinary people.

For the first time in his life he opened his heart and showed all four of us his vulnerability. He finished with an apology for his behavior and asked for our forgiveness.

"I hope you still love me," he said to the kids.

John answered first. "Dad, I will always love you. But I can't respect you any more."

Two weeks later John left for Germany to attend school in Hanover as he had done every spring. It was the last time he would see his dad.

During the weeks that followed, I felt crushed, betrayed, abandoned, and angry. I began keeping a journal, writing into the morning hours. I was a zombie, barely functioning with little sleep or food. I had been cheated on and was overwhelmingly jealous. I stewed over gnawing questions. What did she have that I didn't?

I began to realize that Frank's disinterest in our sex life had little to do with the antidepressants he was taking. I was mad at Susan for betraying our friendship and stealing my husband. I was angry with Frank for destroying the world we so deliberately and diligently built together. I felt sad because the illness was controlling Frank's life. I was frustrated over my inability to convince him to try stronger medicine or go to another doctor. I asked myself over and over again why wasn't Dr. Chuprevich prescribing lithium, the only effective medicine for manic depression at the time, and counseling him more.

I agonized over the loss of a healthy, witty, faithful, and responsible husband. I ached for his strong arms around my waist and our conversations about politics, literature, and legal issues. I missed the clippings from newspapers and magazines that he'd bring to me, the Madame Butterfly and La Boheme he would play on the stereo, or the poetry he would read out loud. I yearned to rehash the kids' schedules with him, to share warm-weather drinks on the porch. I dreamed about our talks of retirement and aging together. I missed the husband who would clear the dishes and wipe the countertops after dinner, copyedit my writing, empty the clothes dryer, and iron his own shirts. Sometimes I even missed the depressed Frank staying close to the house and doing chores, like chasing stray bats with a broom, killing spiders on the ceiling, and setting mousetraps in the basement.

Within weeks after his move, Frank regretted his decision, but was too proud to "come crawling back," as he put it.

"You would never let me forget," he claimed. He said he missed the hardwood floors he had re-finished when we first moved into our spacious house. He reminisced about the playroom he had built for the children, which also served as his gym and his workshop. Most of all he missed the kids.

"I know I cannot take care of them in my state of mind, but I cannot live without them either," he said.

The solution seemed simple. "Give up Susan and come back home," I said.

"I can't explain the grip she has on me. I tried to leave her several times, but couldn't do it," he said. "I don't even love her, not really. She is too short, too serious, and talks too much."

For the first time in years, Frank began to open up and talk to me about his true feelings and his frustrations. That spring Frank stopped by the house often, during his lunch hour or after work, to talk about his regrets, the missed opportunities, and his sadness. Once he described his predicament this way. "I feel like I am driving 100 miles an hour and seeing the cliff ahead, but I am unable to stop."

While his revelations were tormenting me, I was glad to discover Frank's soft side. By being a sounding board, I thought I could help him sort out his emotions. I was eager to prevent more setbacks for him. By leaving the door open, I hoped to win him back and save our family. I never questioned whether he was using or abusing me during those months or whether I had suddenly become a masochist.

Many nights I tossed and turned, frightened about the challenges awaiting me when the day dawned. Mentally and physically exhausted, I felt like crawling into a hole but I had to face the mundane: the laundry, getting the kids up and off to school, taking them to swim-team practice, grocery shopping, cooking.

"What is happening to Dad?" Ayla would ask.

"Is he going to be okay by himself?" Joe would chime in.

They knew Frank was depressed and seeing a doctor, but we never called it "mental illness." I had no answers to their questions.

Our lifestyle changed quickly. Keeping two households meant less money to live on. We had to sacrifice meals out, trips to Chicago, the purchase of large items. The worst problem was the psychological scars this separation would leave on the children. Joe, at 11, was confused and forlorn.

"Will Dad ever come back?" he'd ask as he eased himself closer to me.

Ayla became more rebellious, staying out late and talking on the phone for hours. When she did not get her way, she threatened to go and live with her dad. John was lucky to be in Germany with his aunt and uncle; he was spared the day-by-day turmoil of what our lives had become.

During the next four months, suffering from guilt and shame, Frank continued his visits home pouring his heart out.

"I was an altar boy, for God's sake!" he said. "I even thought of becoming a priest. How could I commit adultery? I am supposed to be an upstanding citizen, a judge, and a role model for others. How could I live a life of lies and betray my constituents, my friends, and, above all, my family?"

He wondered out loud why he couldn't have done things right – getting divorced first, then starting another relationship.

"I owe you so much. You put me through law school. You sacrificed your journalism career to move to this small town," he said. "You gave me three beautiful children and stood by me when I was so sick. How could I do this to you?"

That was a good question. And why was he still dumping on me? Why was I taking it? I decided to continue listening, realizing he was sick and tormented and hoping that vocalizing his confusion might clarify his problems. I kept hoping. I knew he needed me once again, and I remembered my marital vow to stand by him in sickness and in health. I could not turn my back on him even though he had done so on me. I was also still in love with him, and I hoped I could win him back. Betty kept telling me I had to do something out of the ordinary to shake him up.

"You have to catch him off guard. Tell him you do not want to see him anymore. Tell him you are dating or going away somewhere," she told me. I could not follow her advice. I wanted to make sure I did everything I could to help him.

I was grounded enough to know I needed a good attorney since Frank was talking about divorce and did not want to discuss maintenance payments directly with me. He had hired a classmate from his Naperville grade school and told me to find someone. I must have interviewed a dozen lawyers, some as far away as Springfield. Most did not want to take my case because they either liked Frank too much or did not want to alienate him.

The only person in LaSalle County who said she would take him on was Marilyn Barton, an aggressive attorney who swore like a man and intimidated her colleagues. Frank was afraid I would hire her. Instead, I decided on a capable, mild-mannered family man who had moved from Ottawa to Wheaton.

Meanwhile, even though he had read a lot about manic depression and knew how important it was to stay on medication, Frank continued to manipulate the dosage.

Now that he was living across town I could not monitor, persuade, nor nag him to keep on his meds. Instead, Frank told me that Susan apparently encouraged him to quit taking the pills by telling him, "Now that you are out of an unhappy marriage, you will be fine." At the time, I believed Frank thought repeating her statement to me vilified him with another excuse to stop taking his medication.

Early that summer, seeing that the antidepressants were not working, Dr. Chuprevich finally prescribed lithium, which takes six to eight weeks to show results. After only three days, however, Frank decided he didn't like the drug because it made his heart beat fast, his mouth go dry, and his body feel fatigued.

"It interfered with my running and my thinking," he said. "I don't want to be sedated." He liked the rush of physical energy and the poetry that poured from his pen during his manic state.

Ayla and Joe said their good-byes and left for Turkey in mid-June about the same time Frank quit taking his medication. The last time I saw him was a few days before I was to leave for Turkey. He stopped by the house to give me the letter he had written to the children. He looked totally defeated and hopeless. He told me how much he missed the children.

"I'm bringing them back in three weeks, and you will always play an important role in their lives," I said.

"You don't know how lonely I feel, how painful this depression is. I am in a black hole that keeps getting deeper and darker," he confessed. Once again, I pleaded with him to see Dr. Jan Fawcett, chief psychiatrist at Rush Presbyterian Hospital in Chicago. An expert on manic depression, Dr. Fawcett was quoted as saying, "Some bipolar patients refuse treatment after deciding that their situation is hopeless or because they want to avoid the stigma of admitting a need for treatment. Other high-risk individuals reject help even more overtly, pushing away everyone's efforts." That was exactly what Frank was doing.

Several years later, Dr. Fawcett, Bernard Gordon, and Nancy Rosenfeld wrote a book that explained that the hopelessness that is intrinsic to suicidal depression often leads the person to reject help, especially treatment. "It is as if the suicidal patient cannot tolerate one more disappointment or failure," wrote Ms. Rosenfeld, herself a sufferer of bipolar illness.

**"The mission of the United States
is one of benevolent assimilation."**
– President William McKinley

9 - Anatolia to America

Frank's burial was behind me as I winged eastward anxious to take my children into my arms and find the same kind of comfort in the arms of my parents. My thoughts centered mostly on John who had just turned 16. Memories of my own sweet 16 came to mind, and I cringed as I realized how totally in contrast it was to my son's. At his age I'd been living with two healthy, loving parents in Ankara and was at the threshold of finding two more such "parents" in Arizona.

Like my sister Nil before me, I had received an American Field Service scholarship to spend a year in the United States. AFS, an exchange program founded after World War II to foster peace and understanding among peoples, enabled foreign students to attend high school and live with American families. Similarly, American exchange students went overseas. In Ankara I attended a private high school where most subjects were taught in English. Few Turkish students had an opportunity to travel to the United States, a dream still nurtured by most of my classmates.

It was early August in 1956 when I boarded an airplane for the first time in my life. A Sabena Airlines propeller plane carried me from Istanbul to Brussels. A large group of teenagers from across Western Europe joined us for sightseeing and orientation sessions in Belgium. A few days later 400 anxious students set sail for America from Ostende, Belgium, on an old, slow ship named the *Arosa Kulm.*

It took our ship two weeks to cross the Atlantic. As we sailed into New York Harbor and were greeted by the Statue of Liberty, the reality sank in that indeed we were in the New World. I visited the Empire State Building and walked through canyon-like streets lined with towering skyscrapers. I had never seen a skyscraper in my young life. The volume and the orderliness of traffic, the wide sidewalks and even wider streets, and the pace with which people went about their business impressed upon me that I was a stranger in a strange land. I was overwhelmed by Manhattan, felt lonely and inadequate, and longed for home. Most of the friends I had made on my voyage to New York left the city before I did. Now I was eager to join my host family in Phoenix, a faraway place I knew only as the home of cowboys and Indians.

Finally, after four days filled with trepidation, I left the Big Apple (and why did they call the city by that? I had so much to learn) on an American Airlines flight to Phoenix. As we approached the Valley of the Sun, I was elated to see an expansive open space, mountain peaks, palm trees, wide streets, and homes with swimming pools.

Once we landed, my stomach churned as the hot, dry desert air hit my face. I stood nervously at the top of the movable stairs outside the plane. As I walked down, I scanned the faces of the crowd and became aware that a husky, red-haired, balding man in his 40s was smiling at me. Standing next to him was a petite white-haired woman wearing a multi-colored striped blouse and blue Bermuda shorts.

"You must be Sel Erder, our Turkish daughter," they said in unison when I walked up to them. Then they opened their arms, embracing me warmly. Many weeks had passed since I had felt so wanted.

My American dad, Joseph Reavley, had moved to Arizona from Missouri in the late 1940s to find relief for his asthma. A widower then, he soon met and married Roberta, or Bobbie, a divorcee with an adopted daughter, Linda. As Joe's dental practice became more lucrative, they bought a tri-level home in a new subdivision at the northern edge of Phoenix. About that same time, they decided to share their good fortune with a teenager from half way around the world. They thought I could also be an older sister to Linda, who was a freshman in high school.

I came to know the Reavleys through letters before I arrived at their home. So I knew they had two boxer dogs they considered members of the family, and I had worked to overcome my fear of dogs. I took a deep breath as Dad opened the back door to their big, beautiful house. Snifter and Casey jumped on me and started licking my face. I smiled through my fear, determined not to upset my new parents. "See how happy they are to meet you," Mom said. I pledged to enjoy my new family, soak in American culture, do well in school, and make many friends.

My English was okay with good grammar and spelling, but I had no clue about slang, teenage colloquialisms, idioms, and the American sense of humor. We did not have television in Turkey, nor had I ever gone on a date with a boy. Seeing 14-year-old Linda sitting on a boy's lap in the family room watching TV as Elvis Presley swayed his hips to loud music made me wonder what I had gotten myself into. Mom was aware of my conservative upbringing. Though kind and patient, she was determined to teach me how American teenagers interacted with each other. She also wanted me to learn gardening, pet care, cooking, and driving.

Dad was helpful with my conversational English. He would explain certain phrases, and then construct sentences with words that had double meanings. He even taught me to crack jokes. When people asked if I would "talk Turkey," meaning Turkish, I would say, "Gobble, gobble." Soon I was the guest speaker at PTA meetings, student organizations, and the local Rotary and Kiwanis Clubs.

Slumber parties, football games, drive-in movies, and school dances were all new experiences. My girlfriends taught me how to apply makeup, style my hair, and flirt with male classmates. To everyone's surprise, Richard Meyers asked to be my date to the homecoming football game and dance. I wore a rose-colored strapless taffeta dress Mom sewed for me. Richard and I danced for hours and had a great time. I let him hold my hand as he drove home and walked me to the front door around midnight, but I would not let him kiss me on the lips. When I went inside, Mom was waiting up for me and explained one of the nuances of male-female courtship in the United States. "A kiss on the lips is his way of showing you he likes you," she said. "You want him to take you out again, don't you?"

Halloween found me wearing an elaborate Minnie Mouse costume, going door-to-door to collect candy, apples, and coins – a strange thing to do, I thought. At Thanksgiving dinner there were 12 people around the table with Dad sitting next to me. As I was explaining something that happened in school that week, he said, "You're pulling my leg!" My face turned red, and I quickly brought both my hands up on the table and swore I had not touched him. The table erupted with laughter.

I celebrated my first Christmas with Mom's relatives in California. With gifts in the back of the station wagon we drove eight hours from Phoenix to the West Coast. At a pit stop in Blythe, California, Dad decided to give a soldier in uniform a ride to Bakersfield. He sat in the front seat between Mom and Dad, and Linda and I sat in back. When the conversation came to his assignment in Korea, I expected him to praise the courageous Turkish soldiers who were fighting alongside the Americans. Instead he described the Turks as ferocious madmen. He said Turks would sneak into enemy tents and attack late at night.

"They are tough and afraid of nothing," he said.

Dad looked back, winked at me and told the young man, "Watch out, there's a Mad Turk sitting right behind you." Color drained from the soldier's face, and he seemed to have flashbacks of Korea. Cautiously he turned around and looked at me, a 110-pound teenager with a puzzled look on her face. Quickly, he apologized and said he had never seen a female Turk.

Little was known about Turkey in the 1950s. The young Turkish Republic, born in 1923 from the ashes of the Ottoman Empire, which had been invaded by several European countries during World War One, was focusing its energies inward, trying to make democracy work within its borders. Few Turks traveled to Europe, let alone the United States. Most Americans only heard of Turkey during the Korean War when Turkey, a NATO member, sent the second-largest contingent of troops to the peninsula. My encounter with the soldier from Bakersfield showed me I had much to teach Americans about Turkey to help erase the image of the Mad Turk.

We finally arrived at Huntington Beach where Mom's brother owned a food and sports equipment stand where we were to spend the next two weeks of vacation. It didn't take us long to become beach bums, and the best part was eating freshly grilled hamburgers at the waterfront stand. The Reavleys were amused by my screams as we rode the roller coasters at Disneyland, the terrified look on my face when Dracula pretended to attack me at Universal Studios, and my surprise at all the life-like mannequins displayed at Knott's Berry Farm. They told me I was like a kid in a candy store.

Linda and I shared very little, probably because of our age difference. We had different interests and different friends, and my being a foreigner afforded me a lot of attention. She was a bit jealous of me and a little insecure about her identity, having been adopted first by Bobbie and then by Joe.

My senior year flew by. I received good grades, served on the student council, traveled, and sang with the choir. I talked about Turkey before any group that would ask me to speak. I also addressed the graduating class and found myself hard put to express the level of gratitude for the experience that had changed my life.

Shortly after graduation, I traveled back East with 35 other AFS students returning home. Along the way we stayed with families in Wyoming, Nebraska, Illinois, Ohio, Pennsylvania, and West Virginia. In Washington, D.C., I climbed the 1,000 steps to the top of the Washington Monument to see the panoramic view of the capital and felt sadness to be leaving my adopted country. The highlight of the trip was meeting President Dwight D. Eisenhower, who held a reception for us in the Rose Garden at the White House.

We sailed back to Europe from New York at the end of June 1957, again on the *Arosa Kulm*. Nil was waiting for me in Brussels and suggested we go to the World's Fair there. She was taking language courses in northern Germany before starting her studies there as an architect. We delighted each other with stories of our experiences away from home and agreed we had become bona fide world travelers.

I returned to Turkey and was given a high school diploma from Ankara College. My British teachers lamented that I had come back with an American accent. With my improved English and the typing and shorthand skills, mandatory for high school girls in the States, I was hired as an administrative assistant by U.S. Logistics Group in Ankara. The Reavleys had offered to sponsor my college education if I decided to return to Arizona. Knowing my father's modest income could not support two daughters abroad, my parents were grateful to the Reavleys for their generosity and hospitality. And I was thrilled to have an opportunity to receive a higher education in the United States.

My second crossing of the Atlantic was via Icelandic Air. Having received a scholarship from Arizona State University, I felt I had to prove myself worthy. I studied hard during the school year, and since I couldn't afford to go back to Turkey, I worked during the summers.

The summer of my junior year in college, I got a job as a camp counselor. One of my responsibilities was to accompany 12 pre-teens on a hike to the bottom of the Grand Canyon. After two nights of camping at Havasu Canyon, we began our climb back to the North Rim in drizzling rain. We broke camp after the other groups left and walked three hours up the dry riverbed when it began to rain harder. The kids wanted to stop for lunch. We spotted a ledge about 15 feet above us and climbed up, huddling together to keep dry. I was preparing our lunch – spreading Spam on crackers – just as two Native Americans on white horses galloped below us and yelled, "Flash flood, flash flood!"

We then heard a deafening noise and froze in shock. Suddenly, the dry creek bed turned into a giant, angry river churning everything in its path. Trees, rocks, and boulders rushed below us. If we hadn't stopped for lunch on high ground, we would have been swept away. We couldn't find a different trail, so we hiked sideways, pressing our bodies against the mountain like goats. The seven-hour hike took 12 hours. Exhausted, we finally reached the top and celebrated our good fortune just as the sun was setting.

I made good grades as a journalism major at ASU and worked on the college newspaper, the *Student Press*. On Mom's urging, I joined the Alpha Delta Pi sorority and became active in student politics. ADPi had plenty of beauty queens, musical talent, and top students but it lacked a political front.

Slowly but surely, I was becoming a typical American teenager. My sorority sisters had a great deal of input on my dates.

My roommate Becky Larkin, an English major, disapproved of Ross Fish, a dark, tall member of Alpha Tau Omega whom I was dating. She did not want me to fall in love with him.

"You can't marry him," she cautioned. "Your name would be Sel Fish."

I didn't feel ready to become serious with anyone, but I enjoyed the company of male friends. David Flaxman, a geologist who was several years older, became a big brother and took me on trips to Oak Creek Canyon, Sedona, and the Grand Canyon.

I did become fond of Marty Lightner and his blue eyes and dimpled chin. Marty was from Ohio, a graduate engineering student who had a great sense of humor and animalistic charm. Years later, he visited me in Chicago and stopped by UPI to meet Frank. Shortly after the two men shook hands and exchanged pleasantries, Frank went home with the hives. For months co-workers teased Frank about his "allergic reaction to Sel's former beau."

With the help of my sorority sisters and a catchy slogan – "Excel with Sel" – I was elected to the Student Senate, the governing body of ASU's Associated Students, and later became student body secretary, a paid position that required about 20 hours of work a week. Because of my good grades, I was asked to join several honorary societies, including one in languages and one in advertising, which was my minor. I still feel a pang for the "C" I received in Introduction to Psychology, which brought down my GPA and meant I graduated cum laude – not summa cum laude – in June 1962.

As a graduation present, Mom and Dad Reavley underwrote a three-month trip across Europe for me. Three sorority sisters joined me for an unforgettable journey that began in Scotland. We traveled across the continent, including a visit to my sister in Braunschweig, Germany, and took a ferryboat from Venice to Izmir on the Aegean coast of Turkey. We spent three weeks in

Turkey as I proudly showed off my country to my friends – a tradition I continue today.

A year before graduation, I had decided to get a master's degree in journalism and applied to Berkeley, Stanford, Northwestern, and Columbia in New York City. Only Columbia turned down my application and Northwestern's Medill School of Journalism offered me full tuition, a scholarship, a fellowship, and a residential assistantship. Upon my return from Europe, I moved into Willard Hall, a freshmen dorm in Evanston, Illinois. As an RA, I was to keep an eye on 30 young ladies, take turns operating the old-fashioned switchboard, and check in the students as they arrived by curfew at 10 p.m. In those days men were not allowed in female students' rooms.

I was enrolled in the newspaper sequence at Medill, which also had magazine, advertising, and broadcast curricula. It was a fantastic, hands-on education, covering county, city, and police beats and working alongside top reporters such as, Mike Royko of the *Daily News,* Walter Jacobson of the *Chicago American,* and Earl Moses and Jay McMullen, of the *Sun-Times.* The latter became the husband of Chicago's first woman mayor, Jayne Byrne

Mom Reavley's advice on how to date young men must have stuck because I quickly acquired a boyfriend. Ian Russell was from London, Ontario, and was in the advertising sequence at Medill. He had a cute Canadian accent and great stories to share. We spent a lot of time together talking, walking, barhopping, and studying. Ian later married his high school sweetheart and lived in an apartment building next door to Frank's and mine.

Mom and Dad Reavley attended my graduation ceremonies in Evanston on June 15 and took me on a road trip to the Black Hills of South Dakota, Yellow Stone National Park, and the Grand Teton Mountains. A job awaited me at United Press International and I began my career as a reporter on July 5, 1963.

As I flew back to Turkey, 23 years and one month after starting my journalism career, I reviewed the critical questions relating to all that happened to me in the intervening years:

Was coming to the United States a turning point in my life? Definitely. Had I taken the right fork in the road by marrying Frank? Yes. Could I have predicted a fuller and a stormier life? Certainly not.

Did I have any regrets? None at all.

> **"Instant availability without continuous presence
> is probably the best role a mother can play."**
> – Lotte Bailyn

10 - Strong Mother, Tough Sister

I was cried out and totally exhausted by the time I arrived in Istanbul on that August day in 1986. Realizing that I would need company for the four-hour ferry voyage across the Sea of Marmara to the town of Bandirma and, from there, the hour-long taxi ride to Erdek, my cousin Vedat Erder met me at the airport. I worried about what would happen when I saw my children. Would I break down and cry? Would I stay strong and keep my composure? Could my children's love sustain me?

The minute I saw them running toward the taxi, I knew I was the luckiest person on earth. Without words, my children communicated to me that the love we had for each other would keep us strong.

Years later, John told me that the smile on my face as I stepped out of the taxi marked a defining moment for them.

"Suddenly, the dark cloud hanging over our heads lifted," he said. "We expected to see a sad, helpless, devastated mother. Even though we were saddened by Dad's suicide, we were more worried about you. We couldn't have guessed you would be so strong, so composed, and so happy to see us."

The next several days were highly emotional, but truly bonding. We cried for our loss, but retold some of Frank's favorite jokes. We hiked to the top of Dilek Tepesi, which means Wishing Hill, where we tied pieces of cloth to tree branches in the Turkish tradition to pray for Frank and wish him peace.

Gone were early morning runs along the water's edge, long leisurely breakfasts on the balcony overlooking the sea, building sand castles on the beach, and rough housing in the water – family activities that Frank had been part of when he visited Turkey. Instead of bridge and backgammon games we withdrew to our condo and talked or took naps. The more we talked, the more easily we coped. Much was revealed during those talks.

John said he realized something terrible had happened to Frank when Nil gathered him and his siblings around her. "I knew it was bad news, and I knew it was about Dad," he said. His way of coping was by swimming at dusk, his tears mixing with the sea, as he tried to conceal the depth of his grief.

Ayla told me about the premonition she had at sunset on August 4 around the time that Frank had shot himself at midday in Illinois. "I was hanging out with my friends, just gossiping and joking around. Then I felt as though a wind had suddenly picked up, and I began shivering. My friends asked what was wrong. I didn't know. I brushed it off and returned to the conversation they were having. It only lasted a few seconds," she said. During the next 10 days and even longer, Ayla could not control her feelings, bursting into tears in the middle of conversations with others.

Joe was upset with the two-to-one vote that kept him away from the funeral. He was suffering from nightmares in which he saw his father laughing and reaching for him, but Joe was unable to reach back.

"I wanted to be with Dad one last time," he cried. "I remember a time Dad once told me that after he died he wanted to be cremated and have his ashes mixed with mine."

"Your Dad loved you so much that he meant he wanted to be with you forever," I said, trying to explain such a macabre suggestion. "He never mentioned cremation to me, and, even if he had, his Catholic family would have objected."

Joe's recollection prompted an important question: Had Frank expressed suicidal thoughts to his 10-year-old? I remembered the children knew that Frank, in his earliest depressed period, told me he would shoot himself if he had a gun. But that was three years earlier. I later read in the book *New Hope for People with Bipolar Disorder* that of those who expressed suicidal thoughts in the year prior to their actual death, 60 percent communicated it to their spouses, 50 percent to friends, and only 18 percent to professionals like doctors and counselors.

The children and I talked about suicide being a major risk in people with bipolar disorder. "Approximately six to 15 percent of all people who suffer from manic depression commit suicide, often early in illness," according to authors Jan Fawcett, Bernard Golden, and Nancy Rosenfeld. "The risk of suicide is highest during the depressive phase or during episodes of dysphoric mania," they also noted.

Frank's profile fit at least six of the risk factors and predictors of suicide:

1. A family history of suicide
2. An impulsive, aggressive, and risk-taking personality
3. Alcohol, tobacco, or drug abuse
4. Severe depression, especially hopelessness and marked sleep disturbances with agitation and anxiety
5. Social isolation, with nobody dependent on them
6. A recent loss or crisis

7. Poor response to medications
8. Suicide in the spring, especially May, or in the fall.

In retrospect, I regret not having been more direct and forceful with Frank. I was afraid I'd be putting ideas in his head by bringing up the subject of suicide. Perhaps I didn't want to think about it myself.

I remembered hearing about families in which more than one member committed suicide, including a family who lived on our block before we moved into our house in Ottawa. Two brothers shot themselves on the high school football field within a year of each other. Suicide among teenagers between the ages of 15 and 19 is the third leading cause of teen death. Fearing for my children, I asked point blank, "Would you think of killing yourself if you felt depressed and hopeless?"

"Never," was their instant, unanimous answer.

"We see how it affects the people left behind. We'd never do such a thing," John said, and the others nodded.

Much of the discussion we engaged in was about our immediate future – what we might expect back in Ottawa and how we should honor Frank at a memorial service around Labor Day.

Frank's sudden death rekindled 60-year-old memories for my mother Selma. She was just 20 years old, talking to her mother in their family home in Istanbul, when they heard two gunshots from upstairs. Selma raced up to the bedroom and discovered the body of her 18-year-old sister Belma who had tested my grandfather's gun against the window, shattering the glass before turning it on herself. My mother's younger siblings, toddlers at that time, also heard the shots. The memory was so painful that no one in the family talked about it. Apparently Belma had found the gun in the basement the day before and hid it under her bed.

My mother had enjoyed a very close relationship with Belma, despite their different temperament and interests. Selma cooked, embroidered, and was surrounded by friends. Belma wrote poetry, romanticized about love, and kept to herself.

"I lost part of my heart when Belma died," my mother told us when my sister and I were teenagers. Selma thought her sister became despondent after her transfer from the private French school to the public high school where she had to learn Ottoman Turkish and make friends with total strangers with whom she had very little in common.

Shortly after her suicide my grandfather suffered a stroke, and my grandmother, complaining of heart trouble, became a recluse. Selma, noticing her younger siblings were neglected, took on the responsibility of raising them.

My father was angry with Frank for making his daughter a widow at age 46 and leaving his grandchildren fatherless.

"Frank was young and vibrant, he was needed. Why did he do this to you and the children?" he asked me. "It was my turn to die. Not his."

Because he was almost deaf in both ears, Father was in a world of his own and found solace walking along the sea and watching the sunset. He often asked me to accompany him and, during those walks, he talked about his fatherless childhood and encouraged me to stay strong. "Life is going to be hard on you and the children," he warned.

I studied my parents' interactions closely that summer hoping to discover what aspects of my upbringing might have contributed to my part in this tragedy. Raised by a strong mother and dominated by a controlling sister, I often felt intimidated by those who were forceful or loud and usually avoided confrontations. Instead of standing my ground, I preferred to remain quiet, to keep the peace.

Had I been too passive in my relationship with Frank? If I'd been more assertive would things have turned out differently? I compared my 20-year marriage to my parents' union of 57 years. My mother, who was argumentative and stubborn, was the money manager and decision maker. My father, always curious and inquisitive, read a lot and kept to himself. He never missed the radio's noon newscast or an afternoon nap. My parents agreed on little, argued a lot, screamed and cursed at each other, but always seemed to overcome their differences. Despite the high pitch, I wondered if theirs was a healthier, more balanced relationship.

Ever since we were children, Nil ran the show in our household. She was the natural leader with a dominant personality, and she didn't let anything stand in her way. I, on the other hand, was mild-mannered, happy-go-lucky, and satisfied with the status quo.

"How did you produce such temperamentally different daughters?" family friends would ask my folks.

"Who knows?" was the non-answer. "But we are lucky to have a sweet daughter like Sel," my father would add when Nil wasn't present.

I was a sickly child, first suffering from intestinal problems, then anemia. I spent a lot of time in bed or on the couch. Perhaps this was my reaction to the emotions that ran high in our household, to protect myself in a cocoon of illness. Nil still reminds me that she did most of the chores in those days. My mother, concerned about our nutritional intake, prepared healthy, balanced meals and gave us all kinds of vitamins. She also made us drink cod liver oil, swallow raw eggs, and get monthly calcium shots.

Nil, though strong as steel in her interactions with people, was a coward at the doctor and dentist's offices. I was astonished when she did not complain much about the calcium shots and surprised when she bought herself a brand-new bike as she turned 13.

"Where did you get the money for it?" I asked.

"By doing chores and other stuff," she answered. Years later, I learned our mother was paying her a lira for every calcium shot to keep her from making a fuss.

My mother instilled her passion for learning in us. "You must get a good education and become more Western than I am," she said. She attended evening classes to learn English so she could read us fairy tales, explaining: "I need to practice my pronunciation." It was obvious she was trying to inspire us to learn English.

In her late 50s she got a driver's license, even though we did not own a car. A great role model as a liberated woman, she motivated us to be the same.

We were a middle-class family, living in a young democracy with an unstable economy. My father worked for the government-run electric and gas company and earned a limited income. Nonetheless, Selma always found a way to provide us with cultural opportunities. She went without a new pair of shoes or a new winter coat so she could take us to the symphony or the opera. At age 40 she took sewing lessons and made our clothes and did alterations for friends so she could pay for our gymnastics and ballet classes.

By the time Nil finished middle school, she knew she wanted to study abroad and needed to learn a second language. To accomplish this she enrolled in Ankara College, a private high school where all of the courses, except history and Turkish literature were taught in English. "I always pave the way for you," Nil insisted when I followed her to the same school.

Nil sought her goals relentlessly. She was the first person selected from our high school to go to the United States as an American Field Service exchange student in 1955. Upon her return from Kelso, Washington, Nil decided to study architecture in Braunschweig, a northern German town not far from Hanover where Torhan Berke, her classmate from Ankara College, was studying engineering.

Quiet, cultured, and refined, Torhan had won my sister's heart so she put up with a lot of hardships to be near him. She rented a room in a boarding house, biked to school, took a part-time job, and studied hard to get both bachelor and master's degrees. She and Torhan saw each other on weekends for eight years. True to family and Turkish tradition, they got married in 1965 a year before I did. Because of work and budgetary constraints, we could not attend each other's weddings, which took place 14 months apart.

Nil also became pregnant first, but that pregnancy resulted in a miscarriage. Her second pregnancy had a due date that was exactly the same as the due date of my first son. Nil miscarried for the second time and could not conceive after that.

I, on the other hand, had two more children, two years apart. Even though she lived 6,000 miles away, Nil worked hard to become part of my children's lives. Every summer she would invite them to my folks' summer home on the Sea of Marmara in Turkey. She would get them into a strict routine of study, rest, and recreation during the first six weeks of summer and then turn them over to me, with instructions to follow suit.

While other children in the resort slept in late and spent the whole day playing, the Yackley kids had a regimented day supervised by their aunt. They got up early, had a quick swim, and ate a leisurely breakfast, often discussing the family's history, cultural differences, and plans for their future. After breakfast they cleaned up the condo and did "homework," learning to read and write in Turkish. They were allowed to go out and play for a couple of hours before sitting down to lunch with their grandparents. When the sun was its hottest, the children had to take afternoon naps.

When John was 9 years old, he spent fourth grade attending German school in Laatzen, a southern suburb of Hanover where Nil and Torhan had settled down. He learned German at school and spoke only Turkish in Nil's home. He returned to Germany every spring until he finished high school.

Frank had never been to the European continent and was curious about his father's birthplace, so in July 1979 we flew to

Hanover to see John graduate from Grasdorf Elementary School, and then visit Wittisheim, a village in Alsace-Lorraine, then under French rule. Nil and Torhan did some research, dug up Johann Jaegli's birth certificate, and learned a great deal about Frank's ancestors before we arrived.

We spent a week in Hanover, meeting John's friends, celebrating his 10th birthday, and watching him play soccer. The five of us then drove south through German wine country in the Berke's Mercedes, staying in bed and breakfasts along the way.

Frank was out of his element and uncomfortable with my sister's controlling ways. They had not warmed to each other. We got to Strasbourg, stopping at cathedrals, museums, and other tourist sites. In Wittisheim, Frank was thrilled to discover cousins he did not know existed, see the grade school his father attended, and visit the cemetery where his forefathers were buried. With excellent records kept by the French, we were able to put together a family tree that went back five generations. Frank wanted to visit Verdun in France where the Allies had defeated Germany. My sister explained there was not much to see there, but Frank insisted, so we went a little out of our way.

Tension continued to build between Frank and my sister as we drove back into Germany. Still, Nil and Torhan wanted to take Frank and John to Heidelberg, Munich, the Black Forest, and sites in Bavaria. But Frank was becoming restless and on edge. He missed his routine and solitude; too much togetherness did not agree with him. He told me he wanted to return home earlier than planned. I was upset because he didn't care about disappointing us, especially John who had hoped to go on bicycle rides and to soccer games with his dad. Nevertheless, Frank paid a penalty to exchange his ticket and flew back to Chicago five days early. Nil and Torhan were quick to point out this was peculiar behavior on Frank's part.

109

Frank made another trip across the ocean to help celebrate my parents' 50th anniversary in Erdek in July 1982. This time he was in good spirits, relaxing, reading, running, and swimming.

Frank did not object to our children spending time with Nil as long as he was not asked to do so. We both saw the benefit of expanding their horizons by having them experience different cultures and learn other languages. We also appreciated the fact that Nil required the children to write letters to her in Turkish. She would correct their errors with red ink and send the letters back. She encouraged, even pushed, them to view the world from a global prospective.

Even now she acts as a tough surrogate mother, quick to point out their shortcomings, criticize their decisions, and dispense advice, solicited or not. She teases me for applauding their accomplishments, small or large, and supporting all of their decisions. In many ways, we complement each other when it comes to children's ambitions. Where I am soft and permissive, Nil is tough and demanding.

During the mid 1980s, Selma suffered from the lingering affects of shingles, an illness brought on by the stress of discovering she had fallen into a fraudulent investment scheme concocted by an acquaintance. She had always been kind and generous and, despite her acumen at managing the family's finances, not terribly business savvy. Nil and I often thought people took advantage of her trusting nature.

When the children and I left Erdek at the end of that sad August in 1986, I knew our lives had changed irrecoverably. The lazy days of summers by the sea would be just a memory.

The day after we returned to Ottawa, I tried to call my mother to tell her we had arrived home safely. She did not answer the phone regardless of what time of the day or night I tried. I called my sister in Germany and learned she had not spoken to our parents for a couple of days. When I finally reached a neighbor, she told me Selma had fallen and broken her hip the day I left.

Neighbors had taken her to a village hospital two hours away, but did not know how she was doing.

Selma, in a lot of pain for several days, was told she needed surgery to place a pin in her hip. She was taken to Istanbul. Nil flew back from Germany to make arrangements for both of our parents' care. My sister became even angrier with Frank and blamed Selma's freak accident on his suicide.

Selma was hospitalized for several weeks during which time my father stayed with a distant relative, Nezahat, in Istanbul. As the early symptoms of dementia set in, he became confused about his surroundings and kept thinking his wife had died, but that no one would tell him. He was inconsolable, eating poorly and needing constant attention. Even though my sister was compensating Nezahat for her hospitality, we were worried she would be intimidated by my father's curt and unpredictable behavior and throw in the towel.

I was mourning my husband, trying to comfort my children, and worrying about my parents. In addition to facing my life without Frank, now I was also terrified about what might happen to my parents.

**"They tell me you are still.
I only see you running."**
– Carolyn Andrews

11 - Memorial Service

Ten days after we returned to Ottawa and a month after Frank's death, we participated in a sorrowful memorial service for him. It was the Saturday before Labor Day. Skies were overcast and there was a hint of fall (Frank's favorite season) in the air.

Eulogizing him were friends from every phase in his life: his childhood, his college years, his UPI days. His law school classmates were present, and so were fellow prosecutors and judges and extended family members. "Frank did not disappear into nothingness. His spirit is with us. We must keep his memory alive," began John Breslin, serving as the facilitator. First, he called on me and the children, then friends to share "diverse aspects" of Frank's life.

After announcing that the children and I had established a scholarship fund in Frank's name – an annual cash award to graduating seniors excelling in the foreign languages taught at Ottawa High School – I spoke about his multi-faceted life.

"He was an athlete and a scholar. Frank had been an inspiring instructor, conscientious reporter, a competent prosecutor, a fair and an honest judge. But his greatest accomplishment was being a good father. I know John, Ayla, and Joe will make him proud forever," I said.

Ayla said she thought her father was "the greatest man in the world. No matter what happened, I knew my father loved me," she said. She missed her father not "for the loss to the community or the fairness in his trials, but for all those little things you don't notice until the person you adore is gone." She spoke of a wish to go back and undo the past. "But I've learned from the tragedy our family has faced that life is very fragile; that when you love someone you may not have time to let them know just how much. And death is so very final. My father died to end the sadness in his life."

John spoke without notes. He challenged the community to learn a lesson from his father's death. "Suicide must be talked about," he said. "At first it was comforting to hear people say my father's death is not my fault. But now I think that with a little more love from his family and friends, we could have taken the load off his shoulders.

"A few days after my father's death, my mom and I counted 20 people we knew who had committed suicide. The problem exists, and we need to do something about it." He apologized if he seemed to be controversial, but said, "I hope my father died for a reason. Let's honor his memory and keep his spirit alive." John's remarks brought a loud round of applause.

Joe, only 12 years old, kept his composure as he read a poem his dad had heard at a friend's funeral. It is by Robert Hepburn.

I Am Not There

Do not stand at my grave and weep:
I am not there. I do not sleep.
I am a thousand winds that blow,
I am the diamond glints on snow,
I am the sunlight on ripened grain,
I am the gentle autumn's rain.

When you awaken in the morning's hush,
I am the swift uplifting rush,
Of quiet birds in circled flight.
I am the soft stars that shine at night.
Do not stand at my grave and cry,
I am not there. I did not die.

Next was former circuit judge, Michael Howlett Jr., of Chicago, speaking about the stresses of being a judge. He directed his comments to the children and to John in particular. "The public demands that judges be fair, patient, and honest," said Howlett, son of a late Illinois secretary of state. "They cannot always be true to themselves and rule according to their own sense of fairness, but must follow the law. These demands sometimes require great courage and stamina. Each task brought before the bench comes with its own blessings and curses. Believe me, John, sometimes love and communication will not be enough for those blessings and curses."

Frank's cousin, Frank Berger, grew up on the south side of Chicago but spent his 13th summer at the Yackley home in Naperville. "That was the best summer I have ever had. Frank was one of the fairest, kindest human beings I have ever known. He was brilliant, but instead of feeling inadequate, I felt smarter when I was with him. He gave that gift to me."

My good friend and jogging partner, Carolyn, almost broke down as she spoke of Frank's athletic prowess. Over the years, we had participated in 5- and 10-K races throughout the county. Part of the poem Carolyn wrote for Frank follows:

They tell me you are still,
I only see you running.
Grief—
You will not run this way
Still, I know you run today.

Larry Lorenz, then head of the journalism department at Loyola University of the South in New Orleans, talked about his and Frank's college days, travel adventures, and working relationship at UPI. "Very early on, I was struck by Frank's openness, his friendliness, his genuine warmth, and goodness," Larry said. As time went on, I came to love the depth of his mind and the breadth of his interests. I shared his heroes. I shared his love for the language and literature. I delighted in his stories. I treasured his wit. I even embraced his politics."

Larry told the story about how he and Frank once hitchhiked from Detroit back to Milwaukee in the dead of winter, climbing fences without the benefit of gloves along the way and nearly suffering frostbite. "We drank a lot of beer together and chased a lot of girls together, including a new UPI writer who had been an exchange student from Turkey and later became his wife. Frank was an intellectual, but he was not a grind."

Larry then read a poem written by Frank. "It was verse such as this that won Frank the poetry prize at Marquette University in both his junior and senior years," he said.

Equestrian

When I recall the farrier who kept
Beside his forge a spotted wooden horse,
I think of when my father lifted me
Upon that graven shape – I listened to
The clamor of the hammer of the beat.
The beat and spark, the image and the horse,
The man and child & each was in its place.
And now when I am old & every horse
Is passing on the way (the rider of
The last a little grimmer than the rest)
I want to board that block and spotted horse
Again, and ride out of my wooden days.

One of Frank's closest colleagues, Judge Fred Wagner, said he didn't understand why people are afraid to use plain language to describe their feelings. "The word 'love' is almost exclusively used these days to describe our feelings for the opposite sex," he said. "Well, I loved Frank Yackley. I miss him terribly. So often a person's virtues are extolled only after death. Save for shortcomings and weaknesses, we are afraid to praise someone while he or she is alive. Perhaps Frank's life would have been different if he had heard the things his friends stand up to say about him now when he is no longer here to hear them."

Fred then read one of Frank's favorite poems by A.E. Housman:

To An Athlete Dying Young

The time you won your town the race
We carried you through the market place;
Man and boy stood cheering by,
And home we brought you shoulder-high.

To-day, the road all runners come,
Shoulder-high we bring you home,
And set you at your threshold down,
Townsman of a stiller town.

Smart lad, to slip betimes away
From fields where glory does not stay,
And early though the laurel grows
It withers quicker than the rose.

Eyes the shady night has shut
Cannot see the record cut,
And silence sounds no worse than cheers
After earth has stopped the ears:

Now you will not swell the rout
Of lads that wore their honors out,
Runners whom renown outran
And the name died before the man.

So set, before its echoes fade,
The fleet foot on the sill of shade,
And hold to the low lintel up
The still-defended challenge-cup.

And round that early-laurelled head
Will flock to gaze the strength less dead,
And find unwithered on its curls
The garland briefer than the girl's.

The room was still after Fred finished reading, and the quiet startled me. I turned my head to scan the crowd and saw anguish on the faces of our guests. Many were from far-flung parts of the country, like Philadelphia or Santa Fe, and I thought of how they had traveled these distances to honor the memory of my husband.

My attention went back to the stage as the president of the LaSalle County Bar Association announced a room in the downtown courthouse would be redecorated in Frank's memory. American Legionnaire Bill Heinz, whom the children called Grandpa Heinz, presented us with a flag to honor Frank's service in the Coast Guard.

After the service ended, my female friends cried and hugged me as their husbands tried to keep their composure. Members of my two bridge clubs had prepared dozens of dishes, and neighbors had put Frank's photo at the foot of the podium, which was draped in black cloth. Flowers were everywhere in the large United Auto Workers hall, once a campaign stop for Frank. He had to be apolitical as a judge, but it was members of the UAW and other labor unions who had supported him most during his runs for state's attorney and circuit judge. I lingered as long as the crowds stayed and was then whisked away to dinner by four neighbors while my in-laws kept the children company.

The following week we placed a bronze marker on Frank's grave. The marker had the scales of justice below his name, the dates of his life (1936-1986), and the first line of another Housman stanza, chosen with Larry Lorenz's help.

Lie you easy, dream you light,
And sleep you fast for aye;
And luckier may you find the night
Than ever you found the day.

We had taken our first step toward closure, but had a long journey ahead.

Grief took hold of my body and soul with a vengeance. Apparently, I had been functioning on pure adrenaline since Frank's death. My back was stiff, my muscles ached, and my head throbbed. I had no appetite, little energy. My nightmares were so vivid that I preferred not to sleep. I did not want to reveal my deep despair to the children. I did not want them to know how much I missed their father, my husband.

"**Enter not the place of despair, there is hope.
Enter not the place of darkness, there are suns.**"
– Mevlana Jalaluddin Rumi

12 - Surviving the Suicide

My responsibilities as a mother were now compounded by concern for the welfare of my parents in Turkey. I felt guilty because I wasn't there to help them, and cheated because they could not be here offering the moral support I had always expected and received from them. Frank's side of the family had their own lives to contend with. His oldest brother, Bob, had died eight years previously, and Bob's widow, Betty, offered advice and comforting words by phone, but she was busy with her psychology practice and horse-boarding business in Naperville. Frank's surviving brother was in frail health; the married sisters had their hands full with family responsibilities.

Yes, there were many friends offering assistance. But I alone had to raise, protect, nurture, and comfort my children. I understood they were suffering from post-traumatic shock syndrome, but I worried more that there was a Yackley genetic disposition toward mental illness. I discussed with them the hereditary tendencies toward depression, the importance of seeking help early, and the possibility of a crisis triggering the onset of symptoms of bipolar disorder.

"It is a chemical imbalance in the brain, and it can be corrected," I repeated, as if reading from the Gospel. "There is no reason one should ignore or be ashamed of a chronic illness." They winced and looked the other way, hoping to avoid talk of such a fate.

Joe was in sixth grade, Ayla a freshman, and John a senior in high school. I knew I had to bring our fragmented family together and work diligently to sustain cohesiveness. My primary concern was to keep the children from seeking comfort in unhealthy relationships or succumbing to negative influences such as alcohol and drugs. Getting them into college was a priority so I also needed to monitor their schoolwork to ensure their intellectual growth. I sounded like a broken record as I reiterated my unconditional love. I reminded them we were lucky to have each other.

Still, the months following Frank's death were nightmarish. Not only did the kids have difficulty concentrating on their schoolwork, but they had trouble eating, sleeping, and participating in sports. Their interactions with their peers were strained.

John's friends, who used to shoot baskets in our driveway, quit coming around. He was unfocused, missing homework deadlines and neglecting the college application process unless I nagged him. Sometimes I even filled out the forms for him. Ayla continued to be stubborn and headstrong, wrote heart-wrenching poetry, and, at age 14, began dating older boys. She kept company with teenagers I did not particularly like. Joe felt uncomfortable visiting friends who had both parents in the home. He was quiet and withdrawn.

I was distressed to see my beloved children struggle with grief, feelings of rejection, and abandonment. I feared the disintegration of our family. My main source of comfort came from Carolyn, who had received her master's in counseling. She jogged with me every morning and listened as I attempted to purge my anxieties.

The first crisis occurred on a warm October Monday morning as I returned home from an easy run with Carolyn. Upon entering the house, I found a note from John scribbled on a yellow sheet torn from a legal-size note pad.

Dear Mom:

I have gone away for a while. I need time away from home to sort things out. I am not sure where I will go. Please do not call the cops or worry about me. I just need some time alone. I will call you in a couple of days.

Don't worry about me. I will not do anything stupid like Dad. Please call school and tell them I will not be there for a few days.

Your loving son,

John

Despite being soaked in sweat from the morning jog, I started shivering. I was horrified at the prospect that John might harm himself. Frank's final note to the children surfaced in my mind. After all, Frank had betrayed no signs of what he was about to do when he called the morning of the day he died. I was furious, and I was scared.

My stomach in knots, I ran to the garage and discovered John had taken his bicycle. I went back inside and paced in the kitchen, figuring I had an hour before Ayla and Joe woke up for school. He couldn't be far from home, I reasoned, but I needed help looking for him. Calling the police would mean notifying the whole town. Besides, John had asked me not to do so, and I wanted to maintain his trust. Yet I wondered if I was being too passive again. Frank's erratic behavior and my naiveté about the seriousness of his situation came back to me. I did not know if John was in danger and could not be sure that he would act rationally. I remembered the brothers who had committed suicide a year apart. I had to find John, but I had no idea how.

I grabbed a light jacket, goose bumps covering my arms and legs, ran to Carolyn's house and asked her to help me search for my son. She pulled me toward the door and out to her car. We drove around town for an hour, looking first in areas where John and his dad went for walks, in the wooded area where Tim's body was discovered. We drove past dozens of homes, parks, cornfields, and the two rivers. As we drove outside of the city limits, I realized the impossibility of finding a person who didn't want to be found. We looked and looked.

I returned home and phoned the families of John's friends, taking them into my confidence and begging them to let me know if they heard from him. That evening he called, and I nearly collapsed onto the floor when I heard his voice. He was alive. Before I could say a word, he told me he was safe and that he needed more time. Then he hung up the phone.

With John in hiding, I fell into a daze and was willing to let someone else make decisions for me. Peg and Carolyn took charge and searched for a support group for families of suicide victims. None existed in LaSalle County, but there was a group called Survivors of Suicide, or SOS, in Aurora, a Chicago suburb 45 miles northeast. Peg knew a couple from a neighboring town who attended the SOS meetings. Trying to cope with their son's death, an apparent suicide, they had been driving to Aurora every Wednesday for the last six months and said they would take me along.

Peg told me to be ready at 5 p.m. Wednesday. She assured me the neighbors would stay close to the phone if John, now missing for 60 hours, called again and that they would keep Ayla and Joe occupied. That first SOS meeting painted a clear picture of how suicide throws people off, and how unexpected behaviors by family members surface. As I listened to everyone's stories, I learned that some had it so much worse. One spoke about witnessing the act itself. Others lost more than one family member to homicide and suicide. They were suffering from guilt, denial, anger, and depression.

Stephanie, our group leader, was a psychologist. Her mother had killed herself on her third attempt. Stephanie said her mother's story was testimony that often there is nothing a family member can do if a loved one is determined to take his or her life. I was impressed with the sincerity of the participants and the free flow of shared experiences, so I resolved to come back and bring the children. I also made arrangements for private counseling sessions with Stephanie.

I arrived home to smiling neighbors and great news. John had called to say he was fine and would be home the following day. The next evening I wrapped my arms around a dirty, sunburned, and bug-bitten son. He had slept little during the three nights he spent in a cornfield outside of town. Why had he chosen to go off like that? Could I be sure that he would not disappear again?

John had wanted to mourn his loss in private, unaware of the consequences of his actions on my state of mind. I suspected he was overwhelmed with the responsibilities of being the oldest child, and I prayed he would open up and share his pain with me. He never vocalized what he gained from this experience of running away, but apologized half-heartedly for putting me through hell. "I told you not to worry about me," he said. I hoped this was his passage from teenage years to manhood. Not so. He would give me plenty more reasons to worry about him during the next few years.

The sessions with Stephanie and the support group meetings, reluctantly attended by the children, brought some relief for me and were a step forward in our healing process. Carolyn and her husband Hans also took me to meetings of Families Anonymous,

124

another support group that helps parents of young people with behavioral problems and drug addictions. Conversing with sympathetic and caring individuals who were also coping with parenting pressures eased my loneliness. But as months inched past, the pain of losing Frank did not fade. It just became duller.

Back in Istanbul, my mother suffered further complications from her hip surgery. She was in constant pain and unable to walk. Nil decided she would get better care in Germany and arranged for Nezahat to fly to Hanover with our folks. The German doctors discovered widespread infection in Mother's hip – caused by unsanitary conditions during surgery and neglect in aftercare. They operated again, removing the old pin, scraping the infection from the bone, and placing a new piece of metal into her hip. Laid up for nearly six months, including the confinement in a rehabilitation hospital near Hanover, Selma had been immobile too long to ever really return back to normal. In the meantime, my sister, in her decisive manner, told me that our parents should live with me in Ottawa once our mother got a little better.

"You have a big house and you are lonely," Nil said matter of factly.

I knew that the daily trek to the hospital and then to the rehabilitation institute after the stresses of teaching was difficult for Nil and had also taken their toll on her patient and kind husband. Overly protective of our parents, highly emotional, and very demanding, Nil began showing signs of depression. Their three-story townhouse with steep stairs would be impossible for Mother to navigate once she was released from the rehabilitation center.

During the fall of 1986, we burned the transatlantic phone lines. "The children would be a nice distraction for the folks, and you need their moral support," Nil insisted. But I doubted her. We just had too many problems. The children were irritable and argumentative, to say the least, and I doubted they would be able to assist my parents, both of whom were in poor health and no longer self-sufficient.

Nevertheless, I felt I needed to help my sister and agreed to have the folks come live with us, especially since Nezahat would join them. I was working at a travel agency three days a week and figured Nezahat would do the cooking while the folks kept each other company. Part-time work was a nice diversion for me, and we needed the income. Frank's life insurance benefits were reduced by 50 percent because he had killed himself. About the same time, President Ronald Reagan had spearheaded a move by Congress to discontinue social security payments to dependents when they turned 16. I had a mortgage to pay and college educations to finance.

My folks had let their Green Cards lapse and needed long-term visas to enter the United States. The process to reinstate their immigrant status could take months or even a year. Luckily, Frank and I had been acquainted with U.S. Senator Paul Simon from Illinois, and Peg contacted him to hasten the reapplication process.

In April 1987, eight months after Frank's death, Selma, Nezihi, and Nezahat flew to Chicago. I was shocked to see how helpless my mother looked in her wheelchair. My father was a defeated man too, having lost his curiosity and love of life and nature. He was worried sick about his wife. I realized I had taken on a very tough assignment.

Before their arrival I had reorganized our living situation – turning the family room into a bedroom for my folks so that they didn't have to climb stairs. Everything on the first floor was wheelchair accessible. The dining room became our family room with the television against one wall, the sofa, the recliner, and an armchair accommodating everyone. The large dining table was pushed against the windows. One friend loaned us a walker, another one a potty booster chair. Turkish friends (four in all) were invited for long visits and backgammon games, and neighbors often brought snacks.

During the nearly six decades my parents spent together, they fought one minute and loved each other the next. They were poles apart when it came to temperament and personality: Father was blunt and uncompromising, often speaking his mind without regard to people's feelings. He preferred being alone – reading, listening to the news, and puttering around. Mother, on the other hand, was a friend to everyone. She was sociable, outgoing, philanthropic, and a gadfly. Strong-willed, she made most of the important decisions at home and controlled the purse strings. She was also a peacemaker, often mending friendships my father had shattered. Now that she was ailing, Father began to dote on her. Noticing that he was downhearted, Mother was compensating for his forgetfulness and defending his every move. They were an interesting study in marital relationships.

What I found most disheartening, however, was the change in my mother's personality, especially toward the children and me. From a mild-mannered woman, she had turned into an unhappy, helpless, nagging individual. Frustrated with her dependency on others, she nevertheless was relentless in making demands on Ayla and Joe, who like most teenagers, lacked patience and compassion. John was in Springfield, the state capital, as a governmental intern that spring, and I kept telling the children Nene and Dede (Turkish for grandmother and grandfather) had contributed a great deal to their upbringing, and now it was our turn to take care of them.

Father complained that small town living was boring, even though our German-born friend Grandpa Heinz came over to keep him company and take him on short drives. Nezihi would try to stay busy and bake bread from scratch and walk across town to share his creation with the Heinzes. He liked exploring Ottawa but sometimes would get lost during his long walks. People in town knew he was my father and either would point him in the right direction or call me to come and get him.

Not all our days were difficult or full of chores. Once a week, we put Mother's wheelchair and our picnic gear into back of the

127

station wagon and visited various parks. Father's favorite was Allen Park on the Illinois River where he enjoyed watching boaters, fishermen reel in the carp, and tennis games on the park's courts. Mother liked crowds, and I took her to the 4-H fairs and small business expos. Nezahat enjoyed spending time at Walgreen or Woolworth's, which was within walking distance of our home. While our Turkish friends kept my folks company, I took Nezahat to Chicago to visit museums and attend concerts.

We enjoyed many proud moments too. John brought Emma, his African-American girlfriend who was also in the Springfield internship program, to attend his senior prom in a town full of white faces. Ayla, just a freshman, had a date too, and the whole family got involved in the pomp and ceremony of preparing for the big dance. We took dozens of photos inside and outside of the house, including under the crab-apple tree with its shocking pink flowers in bloom.

Ayla wore a girlish, pink hoop-skirted gown, and Emma looked lovely in a lavender tulle dress. Each carried bouquets of fresh flowers. The boys rented tuxes, and I pinned boutonnières on their lapels. John, ever the clown, folded up the cuffs of his tuxedo pants to draw attention to his teal blue, high-top All-Star canvas shoes. Selma and Nezihi were charmed by Emma's efforts to speak a bit of Turkish. Off they went in a limousine as we waved from the front porch.

A few weeks later, John finished his internship and came home for his graduation. A politics buff even as a teenager, he had applied to the People to People Student Ambassador Program, in which high school students traveled to the then-Soviet Union, under communist rule, to learn about this mysterious and powerful rival to the United States. I scraped together enough money and paid the program fees as a high school graduation gift. John and students from across the United States visited Moscow and several of the Soviet Republics. In Baku, Azerbaijan, his Turkish enabled him to communicate with the locals who took some of the students to the only tavern in town. At the end of the evening they were presented with a huge tab, which John settled by giving away his blue jeans.

I returned home from an SOS meeting in Aurora one Wednesday evening to discover my father had fallen on our front steps and broken his arm. In great pain, he began to panic. Ayla was away at a speech tournament and Nezahat spoke no English. So it fell upon Joe to figure out what to do. While neighbors called for an ambulance, Joe spoke calming reassurances in Turkish into Dede's good ear and accompanied him to the hospital. Just 13, Joe maintained his cool and translated as doctors took X-rays, placed a cast on Nezihi's arm, and gave him pain killers. My father's physical recovery was swift, but the injury, causing him such shock and pain, seemed to exacerbate his creeping dementia. Nearly deaf, Nezihi was already isolated. As he became more and more bewildered, he crept deeper into his shell.

Mother had progressed from the wheelchair to a walker and, with the help of the physical therapist twice a week, I hoped she would get along with just a cane. She knew enough English to understand the therapist's instructions. He showed her several easy exercises to strengthen her leg muscles, but she was not motivated enough to do it on her own, even in the clinic. She was putting very little effort into becoming agile. When I asked her if the exercise was causing her pain, she said, "No, they are hard to do, that's all." After a dozen sessions the therapist told me not to waste my money.

We tried to settle into a routine that summer. Ayla worked as a lifeguard at the city pool, and Joe attended soccer camp at the YMCA. I was enjoying the travel business, making contacts with corporate clients, and thinking about increasing my hours to 25 a week, when Nezahat decided it was time for her to return to Istanbul after spending nine months in Germany and the United States caring for my mother and father. She seemed happy in Ottawa, comfortable in her large, well-lit room and enjoying my mother's company, but she missed her own family. As I helped her pack the extra-large suitcase we had purchased for all the items she had bought, I was overwhelmed with the realization that I would now be the sole caretaker of my octogenarian parents, who required around-the-clock attention, and my teenage children, who needed constant supervision.

Having returned from his trip abroad, John began to prepare for his freshman year at Northwestern University, my alma mater. Before setting off in September, he wanted to see Emma, who had already started classes at the University of Illinois in Champaign. Emma was a good influence on him; she encouraged his interest in politics and travel and had a knack for putting him in his place if he became cocky. But I sensed the relationship was lopsided. John seemed to pursue her with a blind passion. While she had had other boyfriends before meeting John, Emma was his first love.

Instead of taking the bus or the train, John opted to ride his inexpensive clunker of a bike from Ottawa to Champaign. It was an attempt to prove both his manhood and his devotion. The 100-mile journey took ten hours and left him sore, dehydrated, and grouchy. Emma was not impressed. Instead, she was cross and impatient. She had joined an all-black sorority and was involved with other African-American student activities. It seemed she had lost interest in John over the summer and was eager to devote herself to college and her new friends. John ditched his beat-up bike in Champaign. Heartbroken and exhausted, he got a ride home from his best friend, David Keely.

The next week, I helped John pack his belongings, and on a warm September Friday, we piled the boxes and bags into the station wagon and drove to Evanston. As I watched the parents of other freshmen move their teenagers into dorm rooms, I felt envy. I had to undertake this quintessential American rite of passage with my firstborn alone. I spent the night at a hotel and attended the parents' orientation the following morning before hugging my dark-haired son good-bye. Driving back to Ottawa, the envy I had felt slowly gave way to pride. John and I had reached this milestone together.

When I returned home and pulled into the garage, I felt the car hit a slight bump and discovered when I got out of the car that I had run over a beer can. I peeled the flattened aluminum off the pavement and stared at it quizzically for a moment before it dawned on me. The mice will play while the cat's away, I thought to myself. I walked into the house, where Ayla and Joe were lounging in front of the TV set, and brandished the can. "Can either of you explain why there was a beer can in the garage?" I asked. They sat up straight and stared back wide-eyed. Ayla spoke up first. "No idea," she said. An FBI-like interrogation followed before they quickly caved and told me they had invited a "few friends" over the night before.

Ayla confessed it was her idea to have the party, and Joe was happy to go along. They figured my parents, both hard of hearing and stowed away in their bedroom, would never even know that a dozen or so people were milling about the rest of our large house. But as happens in small towns when word gets out about a party, dozens of kids showed up at our house with six packs of beer.

"It got totally out of hand, and we got scared," Ayla said. Luckily, a neighbor arrived as the party became raucous and threatened to call the cops before everyone left.

"At one point, Dede woke up, came into the kitchen, and began jabbing his fingers into the chest of Alan, a tall football player at the high school," Ayla said. "He was mumbling something half in Turkish, half in German. But he doesn't seem to have any recollection of it today. I think he thought he was having a nightmare."

I went into my mother's room. "Where were you when all of this was going on last night?" I asked.

"I was here but sworn to secrecy," she said.

Tough regulations were introduced after that episode. I enforced a curfew earlier than those of their friends', and if they missed it, the next time they went out they had to be in twice as early. They also had to give me a good-night kiss when they got home so I could check their breath for liquor. I never smelled any but I knew it wasn't necessarily because they weren't drinking.

Ayla and Joe spent less and less time at home. I sensed a growing impatience between the children and their ailing grandparents. Mother began to insist she and Nezihi return to Turkey. Father missed the summers in Erdek and his backgammon games "with real players," he said.

"We have to return home. We want to die on Turkish soil."

I respected that desire. But Turks take care of their elders at home, and extended families are the norm, not the exception. My own grandmother, for example, moved in with my parents when my aunt took a job overseas. My father's widowed sister stayed with us while her son completed his compulsory military service.

Our circumstances were different, however. My sister was in Germany, I was in the United States, and we had no other siblings. Then Nil thought of Emine, a woman my mother had taken in when she was orphaned as a little girl. My mother's kindness a half-century before would prove providential.

**"The good life is one inspired by love
and guided by knowledge."**
– Bertrand Russell

13 - Good Lives End

Emine's mother had died when she was ten years old, and her father, a destitute laborer, could not provide for four children. As was the custom in Turkey in those times, better-off families took such children from impoverished families into their homes, often to work as nannies. My mother was so moved by Emine's plight she accepted her into the fold years before my sister and I were born.

Emine eventually played an important role in our daily lives during our early years. She had never been to school and resisted my mother's attempts to teach her how to read and write. Still, everyone knew Emine was a very smart girl. When she came of age, my folks arranged for her to be married, common practice among the rural families of Turkey. Emine quickly became a capable homemaker and a compassionate mother. Through the years, she kept in touch with my mother, who sent gifts and cash for her and her children at holidays. My sister and I continue to assist Emine to this day.

Eventually, Emine was widowed, moved in with her daughter and son-in-law, and cared for the grandchildren while her daughter worked. Once the grandchildren grew up, she returned to her unheated, dirt-floor shack in a small village in Thrace, the European territory of Turkey and 600 miles from Ankara where my folks lived. With one son a drifter and the other one perpetually unemployed, Emine spent her meager income from social security on the family. She was penniless. My mother would sometimes send for her, and she would make the long bus trip from her village across the Sea of Marmara to Erdek in the summer. She was respectful toward my mother and treated Nil and me with great warmth.

When Selma and Nezihi decided to spend their final years in their Ankara home, my sister convinced Emine to move into our parents' spacious condominium and become their caregiver. At the time, she was in her mid-60s and in good health. She had her own bedroom, central heating, a modern kitchen, and shopping right outside the door. She walked everywhere, and in the Muslim tradition, prayed five times a day. She tended to my parents and cooked their meals. We paid her a stipend and hired another woman to do the cleaning, laundry, and other housework. Emine accompanied my parents to Erdek in summer of 1988, the last time they were able to make the 10-hour journey by car.

Meanwhile, my mother, a realist, knew her years were numbered and did not want her two daughters to quibble over their inheritance. It still stung her that many of the family's heirlooms had gone to her younger brother, because he had been the favorite of Sudiye, my grandmother, and to her younger sister, because she was divorced.

So my parents divided up their real estate and personal property as evenly as they could. They put the condo in Ankara in my name, while Nil inherited the summer bungalow in Erdek and the three-flat rental property, lovingly built by my father in the 1950s in a suburb of Ankara.

Thanks to Emine's excellent care of our parents, both Nil and I were spared excessive feelings of guilt. I made annual trips to visit my mother and father. Nil traveled to Turkey several times a year not only to see the folks, but also to give Emine time off to visit her family.

Emine, who wore the traditional headscarf of devout Muslims, found it difficult to cope with my father's increasing dementia and paranoia. When he became ornery and said nasty things to her, she would run to my mother and say, "You better outlive Nezihi, because I won't stick around to take his abuse after you are gone."

My mother, though physically frailer, must have taken this warning to heart. She survived my father by a year.

My father died in his sleep on December 16, 1989. He was either 89 or 91 years old, we are not sure. The Ottoman Empire used the Islamic lunar calendar at the turn of the last century, and records in small towns were not carefully kept. When Turkey adopted the Gregorian calendar, as we do in the West, a year or two may have been lost in the translation. I also remember my uncle telling me in the 1960s that he recorded Nezihi's age as younger so he could avoid the military draft. "I did not want him to enlist during World War One. I could not stand losing another brother to war," my uncle said. As it turned out, my father served in the Turkish Navy as a young officer and was recalled to duty for a second time during World War II.

My father's death was not a surprise. Ayla took the call from my cousin Vedat who phoned from Turkey with the news, and despite her grief, she was unable to cry. She dealt with her grandfather's death, as he had with her father's, through poetry.

The Setting Sun

I'd catch up to him
On those long walks to the sunset.
'Dede,' I'd call in my mother's tongue.
'Wait for me!'
And he'd turn and smile
With the gold ball of fire
Fiercely shining behind him.
I'd run as fast as my legs
Would carry me and when
I'd make it to his open arms
I could see love rushing through
His dark blue eyes.
We'd join hands walking
And singing songs from his childhood.
He always loved the setting sun,
His favorite time of day.
'The world's ready to sleep,'
He'd explain, 'and there is nothing so
Peaceful as sleep, my Ayla.'

When the sun set for my grandfather,
I didn't weep.
I only sat silently staring out into
A world of dark,
At the night of peaceful sleep.

My mother became a lost soul after her husband of 57 years left her side. She had no one to care for, pick on, talk to, eat with, and lay down next to at night. During the year following his death, she suffered a series of small strokes that made speaking difficult. In good weather, she sat on the balcony of her sixth-floor apartment or was wheeled by Emine to a nearby park. During the winter, she sat by the floor-to-ceiling windows in the living room watching the snowfall and listening to classical music. She was confined to a wheelchair and became more dependent on Emine. Frustrated by her inability to speak, she became jealous and resentful of Emine who, when visitors came, acted as the lady of the house. She was unlike the gracious woman I had always known.

I was heartbroken during my last visit as I realized she was preparing to die. But it seemed she was doing it in her thoughtful way: slipping away slowly to give us time to adjust, to accept. During Nil's Christmas visit of 1990, Mother took a turn for the worse. After the doctor made a house call, her condition improved so Nil went back to Germany to begin a new semester of teaching. Within three weeks it became apparent that Selma was ready to go. Like my father, she wanted to die at home. Emine and Vedat were at her side as she slipped into her final sleep on January 28, 1991.

I did not feel bad about missing my father's funeral because I had visited him two weeks before his death. I would have been a source of comfort to my mother but I knew that returning to Turkey and leaving Ayla and Joe home alone would have been a hardship for me. However, I really wanted to attend my mother's funeral, especially since Nil was so despondent after her passing. It was the start of the first Gulf War in neighboring Iraq, and many airlines cancelled their flights to Turkey. I was unable to make the journey, and my mother reached her final resting spot without me present.

On the 10th anniversary of my mother's death, Ayla and I were in Ankara. We prepared the traditional mourning dish of *helva*, made of farina, butter, sugar, water, and pine nuts, and visited Samime Altinbas, my mother's best friend. Mrs. Altinbas a refined woman who referred to her husband in the polite form throughout their long marriage, told us about her first encounter with Selma when they were both newlyweds and their husbands worked for the same company. She finished her account of their lifelong friendship by talking about Selma's last day on earth and the day of her *cenaze,* or Muslim burial.

"It was one of the coldest Januarys I can remember, and the ground was completely frozen over. None of Selma's long-time friends came to pay their respects, because they feared going out in that weather," Samime said.

"I too was afraid I might slip and fall on the slick pavement or at the cemetery," she continued. "But I could not bear the thought that Selma – who had been so kind to so many, who had been beloved while she was alive – would leave this world for the other one without her best friend bidding her farewell."

A day does not go by that I don't think of my mother, my father, and my husband. I still use Selma's sewing box and her crystal & silver toilette set and wear her jewelry. Every day I look at my great-grandparents' photos matted and framed by Frank and hanging in my bedroom. I have a chair by the window in my Chicago apartment that overlooks Oak Street Beach. The children and I call it Dede's chair because that's exactly where he would have sat watching the lake if he were alive today.

When I am in Ankara, I sit by the window and remember my childhood and the love my parents extended to me all of my life. A few years ago I wrote the following entry in my journal:

It is 4 a.m., and sleep escapes me. I am sitting in my father's chair, at my parents' condo in Ankara, Turkey, seven thousand miles from my Chicago home. They have been dead a dozen years, but I still can hear my mother urging me to pay a visit to the neighbors and my father declaring me his "angel" because I have just given him a bath. Tears stream down my cheeks. They left me this condo, and I cannot rent or sell it. After all, this had been their home for the final 30 years of their lives. I feel their spirit enveloping me and watching over Ayla, who has made this her home since June 2000.

For decades, I visited my folks here; now I am my 30-year-old daughter's guest. Ayla sleeps soundly in one of the bedrooms, having left her favorite city, the "City by the Bay," to work at a job that pays her half as much in a visually unattractive capital. She says she has made a commitment to learn more about her motherland.

Earlier in the evening, she shared with me a feature article she has written for Reuters about camel wrestling in western Turkey. She talks about Turkey's reluctance to relinquish its Asian heritage as it pursues European Union membership. I realize I have the same reluctance. Having lived in the United States for the last 45 years, I have become Americanized but cannot relinquish my Eastern values or ignore my roots. Did my daughter inherit the same mystical attachment to this culture? Did those lazy childhood summers by the sea leave her thirsty to learn more?

She asks me question after question about my parents, grandparents, and great-grandparents. She listens intently. Then she challenges me once again to write a book about my life. She wants me to tell it all: learning a new language, leaving my parents behind at age 16 to live with strangers in a brand new city 8,000 miles away. She wants me to talk about my first kiss, my dating experiences, college life, my professional career, and the courtship with her dad. She wants to know how we managed on my salary while Frank attended law school, how I managed his political campaigns. We talk about her father's bipolar illness with sadness and his subsequent suicide with resentment. "How did you cope with everything? How could you stand our rebellious teenage years?" she asks.

It was my kismet, my destiny, I tell her. I was put into a boat, which I steered from Anatolia to America through sunshine and high seas — exhilarated at times and exhausted at others. My life and my boat left ripples in the sea that caressed other boats and other lives. Ayla's fate was to travel in the opposite direction. I can only hope that her storms will not be as violent and the sun will always shine upon her. Hopefully she will be even stronger than her mother and her grandmother.

"Life is before us. Love is within."
– Michael Dennis Browne

14 - Romance and Friendships

Three years after his suicide, I was still very much in love with my late husband. Frank was the first man I had ever loved, and I thought he might well be the last. Caring for my children and managing my career occupied my days, and my nights – well, I couldn't think of a single soul in Ottawa I would spend those with. Dating was the last thing on my mind.

Unbeknownst to me, a handsome Southern gentleman who was a customer at the travel agency had been asking a lot of questions about me. Howard owned a lumber mill in North Carolina and was supplying protective wooden crates to a manufacturer in Ottawa. He usually spent two weeks in Illinois and apparently was looking for companionship. With the help of my co-workers, he persuaded me to have dinner with him, during which he told about his separation from his wife. They were in the process of getting a divorce, he said.

Soon I was enjoying his company, amused by the tales of his two grown children, his business, and the talents of his dog. He seemed to share everything with me and expressed interest in every aspect of my life. Howard couldn't have been more different than Frank. He was imbued with Southern manners and conservative political views. At six feet two inches tall, he was a bit portly, drove a luxury car, and had absolutely no interest in sports. I was dismayed that he preferred watching television to hiking in the woods; that he did not read books nor engage in intellectual conversation. But he was obviously enamored of me, and that won me over. "His face lights up every time he looks at you," friends told me.

Howard rekindled my love of dancing and took me to various LaSalle County nightclubs where we enjoyed live music. A tender lover, he was attentive to my needs. He was also an excellent travel companion, and we spent time in Chicago and San Francisco.

Howard kept a low profile in Ottawa. He rejected my suggestion he join the Chamber of Commerce and avoided attending large social functions with me. I respected his need for privacy and realized having someone dote on me a couple of weeks a month was just the right amount of attention. I knew I wouldn't marry Howard.

Other friends continued to be a source of strength. My jogging partner Carolyn, the counselor, still listened to my troubles and found ways to calm my nerves, convincing me I would survive raising three children on my own. Her husband Hans, an administrator at the nearby community college, often gave me a hand with the chores.

Elizabeth Thornton, a single mother of two sets of twins, was my breakfast buddy and, over steak and eggs, shared her philosophy of raising children. Elizabeth took me to her family's summer home in Tawas, Michigan. Subsequently, she had moved to Santa Fe and insisted the children and I spend our first Christmas after Frank's death with her away from Ottawa. That trip started a family tradition that continues to the present day. Almost every Christmas my children and I escape the Illinois winter and vacation in a new location.

Caroline Daughterity had a son who was a year younger than Joe, so we enjoyed getting together and letting the boys play, while she and I worked on our favorite hobbies. She spent nearly a month helping me refinish a grand piano I had purchased from a neighbor. Caroline trusted no one. She made a habit of driving her babysitters home. "I don't want to give my neighbors a reason to talk or question my husband's good reputation," she said. She queried me about my relationship with Howard and decided there was something "fishy about him," as she put it.

"He is monopolizing you and is not willing to socialize with your friends," Caroline observed. "And why hasn't he invited you to North Carolina?" I had believed Howard when he told me that in North Carolina a couple had to be separated for a year before they could file for divorce. But Caroline suggested Howard might not have been planning a divorce. She encouraged me to hire a private investigator and even recommended a name. But I didn't need an investigator. With my reporter's training and instincts, I could learn the truth myself.

The travel agency's Rolodex had plenty of information on Howard, including his work and home addresses back in North Carolina and his phone numbers. One evening I called his home there and asked to speak to Mr. Spears. A woman with a Southern accent asked, "My husband or my son?" She sounded like a wife and a mother secure in her roles. I hung up the phone quickly, embarrassed that I had been driven to such measures.

I was furious at Howard and disgusted with my own naiveté. The devastation I felt four years earlier when I discovered Frank's affair came back, though not as intensely.

I confronted him that evening. He insisted that he intended to divorce his wife, that they had a lousy marriage. They had not had sex in years, and he did not even like her, he said. He swore he loved me. He didn't understand why I could not continue seeing him.

"You wouldn't have given me the time of day if you had known the truth," Howard said. And he was right. I would never knowingly be "the other woman" in a love triangle. Our brief romance had come to an end.

In the quiet aftermath of Howard's exit from my life, I found myself with empty nest syndrome. John and Ayla were at Northwestern University in Evanston, Joe would be leaving for college in a few months, and my four-bedroom house seemed empty. I knew I could earn a decent living in Chicago, but my ties to Ottawa ran deep. I had spent nearly 25 years of my life there and was very much a part of the community.

I was honored that the people of Ottawa had elected me to the elementary school board, where I served for nine years. Area residents had kept me as their Democratic Party precinct committeewoman for 12 years. I served on the board of the Salvation Army and LaSalle County's Cancer Society. I was the first woman in Ottawa to chair the United Fund charity drive. Years later, the managing editor of the *Ottawa Daily Times*, our local newspaper, reminded me of the speech I made when I was elected as the first female president of the board of the Young Men's Christian Association, or YMCA. "I am not young, I am not a man, and I am not Christian," I joked to the audience as I accepted the gavel.

The Ottawa Jaycees had honored me with their Distinguished Service Award in 1975 and the following year submitted my name to a state competition where Illinois Jaycees named me one of Ten Outstanding Young Persons in 1976. I still cherish the photo of then-Governor Dan Walker handing me the plaque. I'm dressed in a traditional Turkish gold-brocaded costume as Frank and my parents look on admiringly. A year after Frank's death, I garnered the highest number of votes, in a seven-county, non-partisan race, to sit on the board of directors of the Illinois Valley Community College. In a reversal of roles, State Representative Peg Breslin, whose campaigns I had managed, was my campaign manager. Ottawa made me feel loved and blessed, and civic activities had become second nature to me.

Early in 1991, my longtime Turkish friend Altan Arsan decided to open a travel agency in downtown Chicago, specializing in flights and tours to Turkey and dealing mostly with Turkish clients. "I could use your help," he said. "You know the travel business, and you speak Turkish. Why don't you join me?" After only a bit of deliberation, I agreed.

The first three months I commuted a couple of days a week, staying overnight with John or friends, quickly becoming reacquainted with the Turkish community, and renewing friendships with my former *Tribune* colleagues. It was like coming home. I worked hard and did not mind the hours. I got to see John and Ayla often, and within a year I decided to move to Chicago permanently. An Artun Travel client who was involved in commercial real estate knew a great deal about residential property auctions. He told me about an apartment building on Delaware Street, one block west of Michigan Avenue that had fallen on hard financial times. He suggested I inspect the building. More than a dozen units were to be auctioned off.

Dressed in a steel-blue silk suit and wearing a colorful, striped hat on a hot June Sunday in 1992, I walked into the Westin Hotel ballroom where champagne was being served as a four-piece band played jazz. Hundreds of people were mingling and looking over floor plans and mortgage proposals, and I felt out of my element, but I figured this would be another first. As the auction proceeded and we got to the unit I liked, I kept raising my placard even when the bid exceeded my limit by $20,000.

"Going once, going twice ... Gone!" I had become the owner of a 1,000-square-foot, one-bedroom, one-and-a-half-bath condominium in Chicago's Gold Coast, a perfect pied-a-terre from which I could walk to work every day. I cashed in some stocks, borrowed from my sister, and sold the four-unit apartment building Frank and I had purchased as a tax shelter in Marseilles, a town near Ottawa. Within a month after the auction someone offered me $40,000 over what I had paid – no comparison with LaSalle County property values. I congratulated myself for becoming an astute businesswoman. Eight years later, I sold the unit for two and a half times the purchase price.

Once settled in Chicago, I rekindled old friendships and made new ones. I saw no need to find a replacement for Frank. I dated for a couple of years but found single men my age often had a lot of baggage from their past. I knew I wasn't any better. I didn't want to complicate my life by taking on a time-consuming intimate relationship. I did admire friends who had loving, thoughtful husbands and enjoyed being in their company, but I no longer felt a void. Instead I pampered myself and did the things I loved, which included traveling the world.

I could discuss anything with Mary Fanning, a fun-loving single parent. Mary and I knew each other in Ottawa, and our friendship grew stronger once I moved to Chicago. A talented commercial artist, she would stay in my apartment during business trips to the city. Mary was nonjudgmental, upbeat, and mischievous. Sharing the same astrological sign, we had become like sisters. We found inspiration and comfort in each other's thoughts, ideas, and company. Since Frank's death, Mary had provided me with many diversions and a sense of independence and strength. She easily convinced me to try new adventures.

When Mary was diagnosed with stomach cancer at age 45, our conversations focused on her children's future while she rested at my apartment following experimental chemotherapy treatments at the University of Chicago. Traveling to Turkey was one of her goals, so Peg insisted I organize a trip. With her doctor's permission, Mary joined 15 of us on a whirlwind trip to Turkey, the first time Mary had been across the ocean. She was energized and inspired by what she saw, sketching Roman, Greek, Lycian, and Ottoman art and architecture.

Upon her return, she created several large canvases of temples and palaces. She painted abstracts of whirling dervishes, the dancing order of the mystical Sufi sect, and the minarets of mosques reflecting in the waters of Istanbul's Bosphorus strait. In the grip of inspiration, Mary also designed and built whimsical metal sculptures. Joy Darrow, a former reporter at the *Tribune*, had an art gallery on the first floor of her Prairie Street home, a historic mansion built at the turn of the 20th century on Chicago's South Side. Joy was happy to exhibit Mary's works. Many Ottawa friends, dozens of Turks, and several of Mary's ex-boyfriends attended the opening reception. Less than a year later Mary was dead.

A couple of years after that we lost Joy. She died from complications of Hepatitis B, contracted while she was an activist in the 1960s, Joy was a feminist well before any of us had heard of Betty Friedan, fighting *Tribune* management for better beats for female reporters. She was also a champion in the civil-rights movement and marched alongside Martin Luther King, Jr. Joy later became the managing editor of the *Chicago Defender,* an African-American daily newspaper. Joy hailed from activist stock: Her great-uncle was Clarence Darrow, the Chicago lawyer who, in 1925, faced prosecutor William Jennings Bryan in the landmark "Monkey Trial," in which Darrow defended John T. Scopes and the teaching of evolution. Joy had come to Frank's memorial service, and I was honored to say a few words at hers. I spoke of her contributions to *Tribune* sisterhood, her fighting spirit, and the Bohemian lifestyle she led.

Three years later another close friend passed away. Farida Khattar, a Maronite Christian born in Lebanon and raised in Egypt, shared my temperament and Middle Eastern values. She worked for the German airline Lufthansa and had fled Beirut during the civil war in the 1980s to live in several countries before settling with her mother in Chicago. Farida had an insatiable joie de vivre and a fantastic laugh, tossing back her head and shaking her curly brown hair as she told an old joke translated from the Lebanese in a voice husky from a lifetime of smoking. She and I would discuss international politics and foreign films, and once a month we accompanied one another to performances at the Steppenwolf or Victory Gardens theaters. During her treatment for ovarian cancer, Farida resumed oil painting, a hobby from her youth. A serene scene of a loosely tied rowboat bobbing up and down in front of a mosque on the Bosphorus shore hangs in my living room. On the other wall are four large installations by Mary of the Temple of Artemis in Ephesus, one of the seven wonders of the ancient world, near Turkey's Aegean coast.

My friends are one of the most precious gifts bestowed upon me. They are a kind of fountain of youth, the source of energy and joy that sustains my heart as I enter the final decades of my life. I have lost too many friends before their time, beginning with my partner Frank. With each passing, I can't help but wonder how many years I have left. So I have resolved to no longer obsess with life's disappointments, and instead I count the blessings that each friend, as well as member of my family, has been in my life. It's part of a quixotic attempt to defy the words of Benjamin Franklin: "Life's tragedy is we get old too soon and wise too late."

"To ignore the facts does not change the facts."
— Andy Rooney

15 - John's Struggles

My return to Chicago after more than two decades allowed me to spread my wings, and I delighted in my newfound sense of independence in the big city. It also brought me in closer proximity to John and Ayla, both undergraduates at Northwestern University in Evanston, a twenty-minute drive north along Lake Michigan.

Though the kids still mourned their father's death, they were no longer the frightened, grief-stricken children Frank had left behind. But the last few years had been difficult. Their struggle with feelings of abandonment, betrayal, guilt, and despair is something people their age are ill equipped to handle. Much to my dismay, John became my biggest concern. I thought he would give me the least trouble, being the oldest and most mature, as well as the most accepting of his dad's illness.

All his life he had been a high achiever. He was student council president and graduated fifth in his class of 280 students at Ottawa High School in June 1987. He had finished a prestigious internship in the state capital and earned a diploma from Gymnasium, the German college-prep school. Dark and handsome, he made friends easily with his sense of humor and relaxed confidence. He was also athletic and rather brainy and devoted himself to his studies and sports.

John was accepted by several of the universities to which he applied, but I was happy when he chose Northwestern over the University of Chicago and schools on the East Coast. I was still in Ottawa at the time and glad he would be nearby. His decision was based on Northwestern's promise of a better financial package and a vibrant social life.

That social life was responsible for a very mediocre performance during his freshman year, as a result of partying late into the night and ditching morning classes. He managed to finish the year with below-average grades, thereby risking some of his financial aid. I took the tough-love tact and told him he risked cutting off my support if he didn't turn his grades around. To show I meant it, I said he would have to find a job that summer and pay rent if he wanted to stay at home.

Instead he came up with what he called a "brilliant plan": joining the U.S. Marine Corps Reserves.

"I can get my college education paid for by the military," he said. "Dad always said we should pay for our own education. He would have wanted me to do this."

"If you make good grades and finish in four years, such a detour won't be necessary," I argued. "Can't you just get a regular job here this summer?"

But there was an emotional element in his decision. Frank had been a reservist with the U.S. Coast Guard and had suggested to John he join the ROTC program when he went to college. Since he wasn't getting much out of school, I thought he might benefit from the military discipline and structure, but still I remained opposed to the idea. I was a pacifist and had lived during the time of the Vietnam War, and I was against my sons enlisting in any branch of the military.

John was not to be dissuaded. So one day in August 1988, I helped him pack his bags as I fought back my tears. "Please God, protect my son," I prayed. The next day his recruitment officer took him to the airport for the flight to basic training in San Diego.

Why had he picked the Marine Corps, the toughest branch in the military? I had recently seen Stanley Kubrick's film *Full-Metal Jacket* and was afraid John, who had a rebellious streak, would crack under the pressure of his sergeants. I wrote to him twice a week and urged him to keep his cool and to make the most of this experience.

"Your Dad would be proud of you, and you will feel like you have really accomplished something," I wrote. He answered once or twice – short, sad letters complaining about the rough treatment, bad food, lack of sleep, and physical exhaustion. He ended his letters telling me not to worry.

I took comfort in fondly remembering his long-awaited arrival into this world nearly 20 years before. John was in no hurry to be born, so 16 days after his due date, Dr. Gerbie decided to induce his arrival. On Bastille Day 1969, the day after my parents' 37th wedding anniversary, Frank and I walked into Northwestern Memorial Hospital's Passavant Pavilion around 1 p.m. In those days, fathers were not allowed into the delivery room. Frank had no complaints, though, and was happy to watch television as the Cubs won a game, beating the Mets 1-0. I was in a twilight zone with little pain because of the slow drip into my veins. At about 6:05 p.m., I vaguely heard the doctor say, "It's a boy. It's a good-sized boy."

John was a happy baby from the start. He took to nursing readily and started on baby food at two weeks. He also soaked up the attention bestowed on him by four pairs of hands, with my folks, jubilant about becoming grandparents for the first time, staying with us. I returned to my editing job at the *Chicago Tribune* when John was just six weeks old, comfortable knowing he would thrive in my parents' care.

With huge brown eyes and long wisps of dark hair, he was such a cute infant that neighbors convinced me to send in his photos to a modeling agency. John's career as a baby model netted $2,000 (a lot of money in 1970) by the time he was eight months old. During the filming of a commercial for Curity Tape Tab diapers, he bit the nose of the male model changing his diapers. It was so endearing the directors decided to turn the shot into a promotional poster with the heading: "How does this grab you?" The photo shoots were located mainly in Chicago's Loop, so it became difficult to continue his modeling career when we moved to Ottawa the following year.

Twenty years hence, John was a boisterous, sometimes roguish, young adult. After receiving his gloomy letters and learning he was getting into trouble at basic training, I decided to call his superior officer.

"John is highly intelligent but refuses to take orders and breaks a lot of rules," he told me. "Don't worry, though: we will make a man of him."

He continued to buck authority and, as a result, was forced to repeat three weeks of basic training. Finally in mid-October, Private First Class John Erder Yackley received his stripes, and I was proud to be at his graduation ceremony. The 15 weeks he spent in boot camp had taught him a bit of humility, discipline, and order, but he still struggled to find himself, and I suspected the break in his education would be a setback. Upon his return to Chicago, he reported to the Glenview Naval Air Station and registered for Marine Corps reserve duty.

With his paycheck from basic training, John purchased a dilapidated, full-sized van upon which the previous owner had painted "I love country music" and a tacky wildlife scene of two eagles flying over a mountain ridge. "I need something to drive home on weekends," John told me, even though we did not see him much. He took out several seats in the van to make it a portable party pad. One weekend he came home with a couch tied to the roof of the van. Pulling into our driveway, he called for Joe to climb up and relax on the couch. When I told him such behavior was bizarre, he shot back, "Oh, Mom, get off my back!"

Boot camp had kept John out of school for the fall quarter, so he was idle until the first of the year and started winter quarter with little enthusiasm. He was working 15 hours a week to earn pocket money and was tight-lipped about his daily life and performance in school. One Saturday morning in January, I called his apartment to find him in bed instead of at weekend reserve duty in Glenview.

"You're supposed to be in Glenview. What are you doing sleeping?" I asked him.

"The Marine Corps stinks. It does not recognize individual achievement or allow any freedom of action," he said, and counted out a litany of complaints.

"Get to the point. What happened?" I demanded to know.

He said he refused to be tested for drugs. "Can you believe it, Mom? Forcing me to urinate into a cup? I am doing my duty. Why should I have to pee in a cup?"

"Why not? Do you have something to hide? Are you experimenting with drugs, John?" I asked.

"No, Mom. We drink some beer on weekends and party a bit, but that's all."

John dodged my questions about his grades and the reserve duty over the next couple of months. Late in March, he was given a less-than-honorable discharge from the Marine Corps for his unrelenting refusal to take the drug test. He continued to drift, and when I pestered him about his grades, he just said they would improve. He came home during spring break in 1989, which coincided with Ottawa High School's break. What happened that week, while I was chaperoning Ayla's German class to Europe, made me apprehensive, even suspicious.

The day we left on our trip, John was driving a neighbor's sports car after dropping him off in a nearby town. On the way home he lost control of the car, supposedly while fidgeting with the radio dial. The car flipped over the median on Interstate 80, and another driver pulled him from the wreckage, miraculously with only a few scrapes and bumps. Our neighbor whose car John had just totaled agreed with him to keep the news from me until I returned from Europe.

Did I believe John's story about how the accident happened? No. "Were you drinking or smoking something in the middle of the day?" I demanded. He protested his innocence. I decided to watch and wait even though I was beginning to fear a successful college career for John was no longer in the offing.

Earlier in the year, I had devised a kind of a promissory note in which he would agree to improve his grades. He balked, but eventually signed a contract that laid out certain terms. If he did not improve his grades by the midterm of the next quarter, I would stop helping him with his tuition and he would have to consider counseling to turn his life around.

John was unable to fulfill his promise to deliver better grades and finished that quarter with two D's and two C's. It was time to lower the boom, but I needed a plan. Once again a friend came to my rescue. JoAnn Richardson, the widow of the state's attorney who had hired Frank in 1970, was a recovering alcoholic who had become a drug-abuse counselor. She suggested we stage an intervention.

On a cool May afternoon, he surprised me by walking in the back door, having taken the bus home. He looked forlorn and grayer than his tweed sweater. He sat on a kitchen stool and began to speak.

"This is the hardest thing I have ever had to do. I am truly sorry for putting you through something like this. I am ashamed," he said softly, without making eye contact.

I pulled up the second stool, grasped his shoulders, and tilted his head up to look into his sad eyes. He lowered his head again and without giving me another chance to interrupt, he said his grades were going to be even worse in the spring trimester and that he'd been arrested by campus police for the second time. He hadn't previously told me that he and three friends had been arrested late in his freshman year for trespassing on the roof of a university residence while trying to pull off a prank. His second arrest came when he was caught partying outdoors in plain view of the campus police. The cops searched him and found paraphernalia, a pipe which John said he and his friends had used once or twice to smoke marijuana.

"Because of my poor grades and this being a second violation, the dean of the College of Arts and Science wants to suspend or maybe even expel me from school," John said.

My heart sank, and I gripped the counter tightly. I was angry. "How could you do this? Do you realize you are throwing away your future?"

"I am so sorry, Mom. I don't know how all this happened. I promise you I will straighten out," he said and tried to put his arms around me, but I pushed him away. I was tired of hearing promises he would not keep.

I looked at this unshaven, weary person sitting across from me, and I couldn't help but remember him at two and a half years of age, entrusted to someone he didn't even know, flying across the continent to visit my American parents in Phoenix. He had been a happy-go-lucky, cooperative, and obedient child.

Before his father's suicide, John was a natural leader. He named the backyard basketball team, which included Frank, The Fighting Pigs and spent hours honing his game. It was just as easy for him to recruit friends for touch-football games on the street as

154

it was for decorating trees with rolls of toilet paper at Halloween. Getting into our liquor cabinet and walking across the frozen Fox River were some of John's more serious pranks. Had I been too soft on him when he was in high school? Did I talk to him enough about the danger of drinking and drugs?

More importantly, what would I do now? I started by making an appointment to see the dean at Northwestern University. "My advice is for him to take a whole year off and get his act together," the dean suggested. "You should make him stand on his own two feet and force him to support himself."

Armed with the signed copy of the breached contract and the verbal support of Northwestern, JoAnn and I orchestrated an intervention during which we bombarded John with our concern that he was in a quagmire and sinking fast.

We told him we knew he was abusing drugs even though he was not yet addicted. I recounted the family history of alcohol abuse and mental illness. Ayla told him how she once looked up to him but now he was aloof and disengaged. Joe said he missed the old John who would shoot baskets and wrestle with him and talk about sports. JoAnn spoke about Frank's hopes and ambitions for John.

"Your behavior is causing psychological and financial damage to our family," I said. "I have two more children to put through college and, under the circumstances, I am not going to throw good money after bad at their expense."

I told him I had attended a weekend retreat, sponsored by River Forest Hospital, and investigated the six-week in-patient treatment program for young people. Knowing full well John was no longer a minor and could not be forced to enter such a program, I still demanded that he go. If he ever wanted to finish college with my support, then he would register in the program.

"I will pay for something like this to turn your life around. Otherwise you are on your own," I said.

John's resistance slowly gave way, and he agreed to give this program a try. I called the hospital the next day and was told that he could check in that weekend. Worried he might have second thoughts, I accompanied him to Evanston, quickly packed his belongings, and we drove to Mundelein, Illinois, close to the Wisconsin border. I drove home in tears.

As he had done in boot camp, John tried to outwit his therapists, but he remained in a safe, drug-free environment, and the supervision was constant. We visited him two weekends in a row and participated in difficult confrontations. One of these involved sitting opposite each other with our knees touching and our eyes never losing contact. John expressed anger at his father for killing himself, anger at me for mothering him too much, and anger at himself for failing to fill his father's shoes.

"When Dad killed himself, I not only lost my father but the man I respected more than any other," he said. "Sure, he wasn't the same person any more toward the end, but I thought he'd bounce back. When he didn't, I just sort of thought – maybe things just matter less without him."

After about 10 days, I sensed an improvement in his demeanor and outlook. Four weeks into treatment, John decided to check himself out with a promise to attend outpatient counseling in Ottawa.

He lived at home for a few weeks before boredom set in. Knowing he would now have to pay his own way, John decided to move to Chicago. While staying with friends, John worked odd jobs, setting up bands, selling stereo equipment, working in a candy store, and checking coats at a French bistro. He perused the free weekly *Reader* for additional temporary jobs, one of which was translating documents from German to English – a task that turned into a frustrating challenge as his computer crashed and the technical language was over his head. His German eventually got him a job at a commodities firm downtown that needed someone who could speak with their German clients.

A few months later, John eased back into Northwestern by taking night courses while working during the day. He had a lot of catching up to do and was motivated in part by fear that his younger sister would finish college before him. He eventually went back to school full-time, again with financial aid, and he received his diploma from Northwestern the same day his sister did on June 15, 1994, the proudest day of my life. Two down, one to go, I said to myself.

John had become a mature, thoughtful young man. He and his roommate, Don DeGrazia, were honored by the Evanston Police Department for assisting them in apprehending a purse-snatcher. Late one evening, the two had heard a woman scream as a man held a knife to her throat, grabbed her handbag and ran from an ATM machine. They flagged down a police car, and with darkness all around, they began to chase the thief who was headed into a parking garage. One of the policemen, in close pursuit, became confused, pulled out his gun, pointed at John, and ordered him to stop.

"I'm on your side!" John shouted as he dove behind a car. The thief then ran out of the garage, was struck and knocked down by a police car and hauled away. During the award ceremony, the chief of police told John that he had helped apprehend someone who had been involved in a series of robberies. Don, who teaches fiction writing at Columbia College in Chicago, later wrote *American Skin,* a gritty novel that is partly based on their exploits together.

A few years later, John demonstrated his thoughtful and sensitive side when he sent me this letter on the eighth anniversary of his father's death.

Dear Mom:
It has been exactly eight years!
For whatever reason, I've thought about Dad's death more on this August 4th. I feel a literal pain in my heart. But it's not a

lonely pain that comes from missing him or an angry pain from feeling as though I was deprived of a father.

No, it's a pain that comes from the fact that my life and this world doesn't have the Frank Yackley of old, a man who exuded confidence in everything he did – the way he told a joke, the way he hiked his pants and crossed his legs, or the demeanor he kept in the courtroom.

He was the one Yackley that made the name somewhat famous and without doubt Joe, Ayla, and my personalities are so vibrant because of his. But you know what? The old Frank X. left us long before August 4, 1986. He left us some time around 1983. And to be frank (excuse the pun), I don't know if, were he still alive, I'd be proud of my relationship with him today. I'd still love him, but something tells me our relationship would be even more distant than it was and that would have made me very sad.

I know that while he was just our father, Frank meant much more to you – he was your husband, the father of your children, a contemporary, and for a long time the romantic passion in your life. But human beings tend to glorify the past, and we shouldn't forget that it was not fun or healthy living with Dad the last few years. You deserved better and still do. I hope you find a man to love and be proud of. But if you don't, I hope that your children will fill that void as best we can.

I love you,
John

Regardless of how often I told John he should not try to take on the role of the father figure in our household, he has done it anyway. Ayla and Joe find comfort in bouncing ideas off him and knowing he is always there for guidance. I look to him for advice and support. It was John who traveled from Dublin, Ireland, where he worked for two years, to be at my side when I underwent surgery in 1999. It is John who helps with projects around the house and manages our investments well enough for me to enjoy retirement. He lives in the next apartment tower, and we often have breakfast together before he leaves for work. It is John who goes to Ottawa on the anniversary of his dad's death to put flowers on Frank's grave.

A man of conviction, especially when it comes to politics, he believes in small government, voluntary welfare, and hard work. A Libertarian since his college days, he and I have learned to avoid heated discussions since we are at opposite ends of the political spectrum. Still, I was first in line helping him with his campaign for a seat in the Illinois General Assembly in Chicago's 11th district in 2002. He knew he had no chance beating a Democratic candidate in Chicago, but the Libertarian Party had asked him to run, wanting to fill slots on the ballot. Because of our hard work, John garnered 13 percent of the vote, the highest among all third-party candidates in Chicago that year.

Considerate, self-confident, and true to himself, he has forged ahead with humor and a sense of wonder. John has become a rock-solid family member and is a sounding board for all three of us. He is a loyal friend to his buddies and an insightful and responsible adviser to clients and acquaintances. He takes advantage of opportunities that come his way and knows when to take risks and when to pull back. His well-planned, unwavering decisions and hard work have served him well. Be Free Investments, his money-management firm, launched in late 2001, at the height of financial market turmoil, continues to blossom.

**"We must have the courage to allow
a little disorder in our lives."**
– Ben Wieninger

16 - Ayla's Suffering

When I found out I was pregnant for the second time, I wanted my baby to be a girl. To make sure my prayers were heard, I climbed to the top of Dilek Tepesi, the wishing mountain, in Erdek in the summer of 1971 and tied a piece of cloth on the branch of a tree. Legend has it that if you trek up this steep hill with its commanding view of a placid bay in the Sea of Marmara, you are closer to God. Tradition dictates that you take a stone from the summit with a promise to bring it back once your wish comes true. Mine did, and I returned the stone the next time I visited Dilek Tepesi.

When she was little, Ayla (pronounced eye-*lah*) hated her name mostly because Americans could not pronounce it correctly. In Turkish, the *ayla* is the halo around the moon, and it suits my bright, romantic daughter. She eventually learned to love her name and appreciate its uniqueness.

We held a lot of hopes for Ayla Jean before she was even born. We hoped she would arrive on schedule and be our Christmas baby – or on my 32nd birthday, December 28 – but her self-determination, which was to become a dominant trait, revealed itself early on. She took her sweet time being born, arriving at 6:50 a.m. on the last day of 1971. I was thrilled to have a daughter, and Frank, never one for social events, was happy to have an excuse to turn down an invitation to a New Year's Eve party.

Ayla kept me on my toes from the moment she was born. She began walking and talking at 11 months, exhausting me as I listened to and chased after her. A curious toddler who explored her surroundings relentlessly, she would climb stairs, crawl through fences, and scramble up on the swivel chairs in our kitchen, tumbling down and hurting herself. A bit of a tomboy, she refused to wear dresses and liked to chase after a soccer ball alongside her brothers. In grade school, she earned first-place trophies on the YMCA swim team and argued with her teachers. As a teenager, she butted heads with me day and night, and as an adult, she now mothers and bosses me around.

The boys went along with most of the rules, but Ayla was always stubborn and argumentative. When I laid down the law, she would yell, "I hate you! I hate you!" Frank was also frustrated by her unruly behavior, but he described her as feisty and urged me not to "break her spirit."

By the time Ayla was in sixth grade and our confrontations were escalating, I suggested we both needed counseling. Like her father, she did not want to go. Finally, I made a deal with her. She loved animals, so I promised to enroll her in horseback-riding classes if she agreed to see a child psychologist. One afternoon a week, I would fetch her from school, drive to the next town, and drop her at a barn where she learned to care for and ride a horse. On another day, I would take her to the psychologist. Two years later, circumstances and Ayla changed once again.

Even though Frank had moved out of the family home three months before Ayla's eighth-grade graduation, together we attended the ceremony that June and later watched her at the school dance. She wore a white dress, white pantyhose, and flat white shoes. Long pearls twirled round her neck, and her thick brown hair framed her exuberant face. She suddenly seemed very grown up. A few weeks later, she and Joe bid us good-bye and flew to Turkey. It was the last time they would see their father.

Ayla felt abandoned after her father's death, and she rejected my overtures, looking outside the home for comfort and company. She demanded more privileges and often was belligerent. Our arguments grew louder and more intense. She often left the house without telling me where she was going. On the phone day and night and out with friends late, she began dating older boys at age 14.

When she was 18, Ottawa police questioned her and two friends about beer found in their car. She kept the incident a secret from me: I learned of it only after she had moved out of the house. She was not as rash as John, but she walked a fine line, taking risks but careful to cover her tracks.

Ayla wore the vests of her dad's old suits and played a cassette of poetry Frank had recited and recorded for her. Sensitive and in pain, she wrote reams of poetry and prose about her father's suicide.

i'll never know

i'll never know what passed through his mind
those last moments before death tore out his soul.
did he scream, did he cry?
did he remember my joy at learning to ride john's bike?
or did he think of rolling pumpkins with his brothers
so long ago on halloween?
i can only imagine the screaming, ripping pain.

*a lifetime of thinking i knew him well enough to call him
   my father,
and in death i can only wonder.*

*i'll never know if he regrets it,
 if there was any escape from his torment.
is he in the heavens above still roaming, brooding,
still in the same agony of depression?
or is he finally at peace with his family,
his life, his honored profession?
the disappointments and the heartaches of being a man
(no, not just a man, he strove to be beyond that)
drove him to commit the act that left three children
and a wife to carry on without the man
who didn't really fail.
we never loved him any less for falling.
we didn't want an idol, we only wanted dad
to shoot hoops, to wrestle, and to read bedtime stories.
he was such a dreamer, such a poet.
rows upon rows of books
on the great depression, russian revolution, and churchill.
poetry by housman, novels by hemingway and faulkner.*

*i'll never know another man as beautiful, as sensitive,
as sad as my father.
as the years pass and i repress my thoughts of him,
to spare myself the pain of remembering,
i lose touch with the man.
i forget his smell, his laugh, his hands so like my own
but i have to live, even if he died.
there's no going back,
i'm the only daughter of a dead man.
he gave me so much when he was alive and
through his death he continued to give.*

i can say i've grown, that i have more insight and
sensitivity than my counterparts,
but i can never say it was worth it.

i'll never know a pain this great.
oh, i still miss him, as i did the day he died
as i will in twenty years.
but i no longer feel cheated and insulted
i only have bittersweet, faded memories of a man and a life
that i hold in the folds of my heart as gently
as i would a dried flower,
seeing the fragile danger of it all
blowing away with the wind.

Her peers were drawn to Ayla, but she could not always keep the friends she made. Two girls she knew since pre-school formed the core of her social circle, and they did everything together in school and on weekends. During her junior year in high school, her long-time friends excluded her from their popular clique. A heated argument bruised the young egos of her competitive and emotional friends, who turned their backs on her. Unaware of or unconcerned about Ayla's need for approval and friendship, the girls did not leave room for an apology. Besides, Ayla was too proud and unbending. Fourteen years went by before one of the girls contacted her via email and apologized for their youthful insensitivity toward a friend mourning the loss of her father.

John was in college now, and Ayla felt few of her schoolmates shared her values or interests. She began hanging out with people I did not approve of, so our arguments and struggles continued. She was an average high school student in every subject but thrived in her literature and composition classes and won school prizes for her poetry and in speech competitions. The following verse, modeled on a Langston Hughes poem, took first prize in a writing competition and was published in the school's literary magazine.

Theme for English III

A paper out of me, Myers
A piece of my soul, my spirit?
Who am I, what am I?
You ask for a theme for English III.

I am Ayla, with the funny first name,
Even funnier last name.
My eyes are Turkish – deep, brown
To match my hair.

I live for tomorrow, but each day
Relive the past.
I am a young woman of seventeen,
Yet a little girl who still cries for
Her Daddy.
Each day I grow more like him
With my eyes, I see what he saw.
I live for him the rest of his life.

I sometimes miss my pal.
Feel lost without her and
Our mud pies and secret talk
There for so long...gone so fast
But I move on and I move up
Wipe my tears, and wish for her
The Best.

When I'm lost, I find myself on Congress
There's Johnny and there's Joe.

When my heart longs for more
I escape and I write and I write.

Here's your paper, Myers.
My soul, my spirit
Too long, too much
It's me, my theme for English III.

Bill Myers, her English teacher, encouraged her to put her frustrations on paper. She became editor of the school newspaper and was on the yearbook staff, which triggered her interest in pursuing a writing career.

High school graduation was bittersweet with only John, Joe, and me in the stands to cheer Ayla on. She won a full-tuition scholarship from the University of Illinois at Urbana Champaign after submitting an essay to the Illinois General Assembly.

Cursing fate for Frank's absence, I helped Ayla pack her belongings and drove downstate to get her settled into college life. She never took to the U of I, finding the classes too large, the campus too crowded, and the students too provincial. "Champaign is just a bigger version of Ottawa. It is rural and unsophisticated," she sniffed.

Determined to transfer to a school in Chicago, she studied hard, got good grades, and wrote for the campus newspaper. In the spring of her freshman year, she applied for a transfer to the College of Arts and Science at Northwestern University and was accepted.

Now that she was on her own and we did not see each other every day, we got along better. Ayla blossomed at NU. She pledged a sorority, socialized with her brother's friends, and took in the cultural attractions of Chicago. She worked part-time to earn enough money to go on trips during semester breaks.

Ayla always loved earning and spending money. She began babysitting at age 11 and became a hostess at an all-night restaurant at age 15. She worked odd jobs during high school and college, eager to become totally independent and pay back her school loans as soon as she graduated from Northwestern.

Ayla became a self-sufficient, creative, independent, and adventurous adult quickly. Her attachments are intense and her breakups heart-wrenching. She is sensitive and loving in her relationships with others, as demonstrated in this thoughtful letter written on what would have been my 28th wedding anniversary.

30 April 1994

Dear Mom,
Even though a day doesn't go by that I don't think about you, there are certain days in the year that you are especially on my mind. Your anniversary with Dad is one of them. I know this is a very personal day for you, and I can't completely understand its significance at this point in my life. But it is also a very special day for the three of us (and this is stating the obvious, I know), because it marks the very beginning of our lives.
I hope that today is not just a sad day, but one where you can happily remember all the beautiful moments you and Dad shared. I have to tell you, as bad as things must have been for you two, I knew that Dad still loved you more than anything. I still think of your love as very special, deep, and oh-so-strong. I can only hope that I find something like that someday.
It is hard to celebrate the day since Dad is no longer with us. It reminds us of how much we miss him and still need him. We must not let ourselves forget that it remains one of the most beautiful days of all our lives.
I think that is the way we should celebrate it. In the years since Dad has been gone, you have done so much for yourself and continued to grow as a beautiful and wonderful woman. Sooner or later it's inevitable that someone will realize how great you are. Then you might begin to celebrate another special day. But this

day, today, will always remain one of the greatest days of our lives.

I love and respect you so much, Mom!
Ayla Jean

In early 1995, she and two friends rented a moving van, loaded it with second-hand furniture, and drove to Washington, D.C. Once in the capital, they leased a converted carriage house, settled in, and began looking for work, mostly waiting on tables at restaurants. Ayla enjoyed the political atmosphere of D.C. and wrote articles for The Turkish Times.

After a year in Washington, she hatched a new plan to move to the West Coast with two sorority sisters. It took them a week to drive across the country to San Francisco, stopping along the way to visit friends. Again Ayla waited tables and worked temporary office jobs until one of my former colleagues from the *Tribune*, Kalliope Fiske, gave her some good advice. Topy, as everyone calls her, was then the managing editor at the *Los Angeles Times'* Orange County edition but had worked at the *San Francisco Chronicle* previously and had contacts in the Bay Area.

"You are a good writer. You should follow in your parents' footsteps," she told Ayla and suggested online media as a good place to launch her journalism career. Topy gave her some leads, and within a month Ayla was copyediting at a website. She loved San Francisco and lived there for four years, moving from one apartment to the next after splitting up with her college roommates.

Restless again, Ayla applied for a journalism fellowship in Germany. The fellowship took her to *Die Welt*, a newspaper in Berlin, re-unified Germany's vibrant new capital. Her German improved quickly, and she enjoyed the print medium experience as an editor at the paper's daily English-language section. She was two hours away by train from her aunt and uncle's home in Hanover and three hours by plane from Dublin, where John was working. When I visited her in Berlin, as I had done in D.C. and

San Francisco, I was amazed at how capable, independent, and adaptable Ayla had become.

She stayed in Berlin after completing her fellowship, freelancing for U.S. publications, including a couple of stories for the Chicago Tribune, which pleased me endlessly. She then headed to Turkey to work for The Associated Press in the capital, Ankara. Her conversational Turkish was charming, but reading Turkish newspapers was a challenge. Unlike U.S. newspapers, which are written in a straightforward style that even a 13-year-old can understand, the Turkish media prides itself on arcane language. Our phone conversations in the early days dealt with the meaning of phrases since she had to read the Turkish wire services and newspapers in order to write for the international readers.

I was amused at the irony of our reversed journalism careers. Thirty-seven years previously, I was hired by the AP's competitor, United Press International, in Chicago, writing in my second language. Now Ayla was working in my hometown, reading and translating her second language. Within a few months, she moved to Reuters, the London-based news agency, and made her stay in Turkey a long-term commitment. Ayla has interviewed prime ministers, traveled with the Turkish military, attended high-profile trials, and covered international soccer matches. She has interviewed hunger strikers days before they died and sat with Kurdish tribal lords in Turkey's troubled southeast. She has seen corpses pulled from the rubble of buildings bombed by extremists. She has written about financial crises, elections, and the run-up to the U.S. invasion of Iraq. She has reported from Afghanistan, Iran, and Cyprus.

After spending three years in Ankara, a homogeneous city that lacked a cosmopolitan air like other capitals, she asked for a transfer to Istanbul. At last, she says, she has come home.

During a NATO summit in Istanbul in June 2004, she was filing by phone details of a demonstration by a leftist group that was wielding broomsticks and waving flags. Police, anxious to keep things under control, exploded gas canisters. Trapped by the wall behind her and still on the phone, Ayla felt safe with her hard hat on and her press badge dangling from her neck.

"All of a sudden this young cop and I lock eyes. The next thing I know, he pulls out a can of Mace, aims it at my face, and sprays me," she told me later that day. Temporarily blinded and in a lot of pain, Ayla somehow continued to cover the protest.

My friends ask if I worry about Ayla's safety. I worry more about her mental state. Will a confrontation or crisis trigger the same illness suffered by her dad? Will she act in a timely manner if she needs help coping? Is she willing to admit her genetic predisposition?

After five years with Reuters, Ayla accepted a position with Bloomberg News, a U.S.-based financial news agency, in Istanbul, ready for further training in economic news. She is becoming a well-rounded journalist, having covered sports, breaking news, politics, and now the markets. She is committed to staying in Turkey a few more years, giving us an excuse to visit her there.

Of course, I would love for her to return to the United States, settle down near me, meet a wonderful man whom she would like to marry, and start a family. But at the moment she thrives on being in the middle of the action. As her dad said, she is indeed a free spirit. She is happiest when she is challenged, and reporting history in the making stimulates her mind and expands her psyche.

As always, I support her ambitions, respect her decisions, and yearn for her as my mother did for me forty years ago.

**"If a child lives with approval,
he learns to live with himself."**
– Dorothy Law Nolte

17 - Joe's Loneliness

In early 1973, I persuaded the Community Hospital of Ottawa to hire me as a part-time public relations consultant, a position few hospitals had in those days. The administrator and the board needed to improve the hospital's image, especially since they were building a costly new facility on Highway 6 east of Ottawa. My responsibilities included media relations, fundraising, and internal communications as well as a monthly newsletter. I was enjoying this new challenge and looking forward to turning it into a full-time position as John and Ayla grew older.

Ayla was a year old and John was three. Frank and I had decided a boy and a girl completed our family. Shortly after I began working, I was puzzled when I missed my period. A visit to our family doctor revealed I was pregnant.

My parents came to our rescue once again, arriving in Ottawa in mid-October, about a month before the baby was due on

Veterans Day. When my doctor told me he was going on vacation the first week in November, I agreed to have my labor induced on October 31st. John's arrival had been induced, and it was a breeze. Frank brought me to the hospital around noon, and Dr. Schmidt broke my water bag. However, nothing happened for a few hours. Then, suddenly, I became light-headed as my blood pressure dropped to a dangerously low level. The nurses took my pulse, and a concerned-looking surgeon entered the room.

Luckily, my vitals soon returned to normal, and Joseph Nezih Yackley came into the world five minutes before midnight on Halloween 1973. At seven pounds and seven ounces, he was a good-sized, sweet-tempered, green-eyed baby. In addition to the love he received from his dad and me, the nurturing attention he received from my parents made him a happy toddler.

Everything about Joe was sweet and easy, even his potty training. I had read somewhere that the quickest method was to devote a full day of undisrupted attention in a confined space. So on Father's Day in 1976, Frank took the older two children on a day trip and left the two of us to the task at hand. We holed up in our large kitchen with a portable potty in the corner. I used a life-like doll to demonstrate the act of peeing after giving it some water and cheered on Joe when he followed suit. We drank a lot of water and lemonade, played games, and talked about the advantages of using a grown-up's toilet. We then ceremoniously threw away the remaining box of diapers.

A relaxed, easy-going child, he was always low-maintenance. I will never forget one day when he was only four years old. He fell flat on his face playing near the basement door. I was packing the last of our suitcases, preparing to go to the airport for our flight to Turkey that afternoon, when Ayla ran into the house screaming, "There's blood all over Joe's face and body!" Breathless, I ran out and picked him up in my arms. He had knocked out his front baby tooth and was dazed but, characteristically, calm. We rushed to the children's dentist, who took X-rays to make sure Joe had not damaged the roots of the permanent tooth that would not come in for another four years. He stopped the bleeding, gave us some pills that would make Joe sleep through the flight, and sent us on our way. For the next four years Joe went around without a front tooth, telling everyone about the accident and how the tooth fairy came all the way to Istanbul to leave money under his pillow.

Joe has been measured and deliberate ever since he was a little boy. Competing with his older, more intense siblings, he fought for equal time, especially with Ayla, who would often interrupt his stories or finish his sentences at the dinner table. He is a river that runs deep, concealing his true strength until he is tested.

Throughout his teens, Joe was laid-back. He was a good student who excelled in sports and music, playing the saxophone, piano, and drums. He made friends easily and, though not a comedian like his brother, Joe always made people smile. While still an honor student in high school, he enrolled in several courses at Illinois Valley Community College, determined to finish his university education early so he could travel the world. During the summer of 1991, he took introductory calculus classes at Boston College. When he was 17, he sent me the following letter.

29 July 1991

Mom:

This summer at Boston College has been more rewarding than I thought possible – in social, intellectual, and emotional ways. I know this program was expensive, but it has meant a lot to me. Thank you very much, Mom.

I'm writing you this note because I want you to understand how important you are to me. When Dad was alive, I viewed him as the greatest man I've ever known. At the age of 11, when I'd ask him if a friend could stay over or if I could skip dinner, his answer was always "Ask Sel," or "It's fine with me as long as Sel agrees." This allowed FXY to never say "no." Therefore, I could never get angry with him. You, on the other hand, would say "no" because Frank never would. I resented your decisions and failed to realize that Dad's answers were copouts. Now I know you had to assume all the responsibility. After his death, I tried to replace Dad with John. He was the only older male around. Once he left for college, it was as if I had lost a second father.

There always was a healthy rivalry between Ayla and myself, which tended to keep her a sister instead of someone like Dad or John. (Besides, she could not make a hook shot). I then began to pull inward and became an introvert at home and extrovert around my peers. Now that Ayla is gone to school, only you and I are left. Soon I will be gone, and you will be all by yourself. You have also dealt with your parents' deaths, so close together. With all these problems, you have continued taking good care of your three children. You have been strong and stable. We are lucky to have you as our mother.

You have the ability to lead, guide, and manage us without dictating. I'll never be able to repay you for the many opportunities you have given me while allowing me to make my own personal decisions. I am grateful for your compassionate guidance and your brave disposition. Great lessons you have taught me.

I love you more than you can know.
Joey

Joe's best friend since middle school was Aaron Miller. They were good students, though they had some disciplinary problems. I figured their childish pranks, like throwing eggs at the band teacher's house and talking back to the tennis coach, were par for the course.

During the fall of his senior year in high school, I received a call from Ottawa's police chief telling me Joe had stolen a pumpkin from a neighbor's porch. When Joe came home, I confronted him, but he denied it. Easily convinced my baby could never do anything unlawful, I phoned the police chief to protest Joe's innocence until he interrupted to say the police had a description of the car and my license plate number. When I confronted him a second time, Joe admitted taking the pumpkin as a prank. "There were several pumpkins on the porch, and I didn't think they'd notice," he said meekly.

For lying to me, I grounded him for a week, which included his 18th birthday. I also made him replace the pumpkin and apologize to the neighbor's children. John and Ayla pointed out that this prank was heartrendingly poignant: It had been inspired by tales Frank had told the children about stealing pumpkins and smashing them in the streets of Naperville 50 years earlier. It seemed Joe was trying to keep his father's memory alive by mirroring his practical jokes.

Joe and Aaron's friendship grew stronger in the final year of high school and later, even though they chose to attend college miles apart. They loved the outdoors and spent two summers hitchhiking across the West. One of their longer camping trips was a 10-day hike through the backcountry of Yellowstone National Park. They carried all their belongings in their backpacks, using tablets to purify water. They bathed in frigid creeks and cooked over open fires. Aaron's parents were divorced when he was a small boy, and his father lived in Colorado with his second wife. During the school year, Aaron stayed with his mother and sister in Ottawa. In many ways I think the two served as male role models for each other as they entered adulthood.

Having become an expert on the outdoors, Joe later guided his brother and sister trekking through Yosemite National Park in northern California. Ayla told me later how impressed she was with her little brother's outdoor skills.

I sensed Joe's loneliness with his older siblings away at school. By the time he was a senior, I was working in the travel business in Chicago and commuting two or three days a week. While I was away, Joe cooked for himself and spent evenings with his friends. When I learned he had dropped out of the high school band and quit the tennis team, I began to worry that his life was too unstructured. Nevertheless, Joe usually stayed out of trouble and kept busy with university-level courses at the nearby community college. Later that year, he was accepted to Northwestern University and decided to spend the next four years close to his brother and sister in Evanston.

Joe had a difficult first term at Northwestern, getting poor grades in advanced calculus and chemistry courses. He enjoyed an introductory philosophy class and informed me philosophy would be his major.

"How do you expect to make a living?" I asked.

"I'll probably go to graduate school," he answered.

Joe was a serious student, and while I was concerned about his choice of a major, I was confident he would excel in his program and thought he might later apply to law school, like his father.

Joe's sense of adventure continued, and he considered studying abroad his junior year. A fraternity brother had just returned from Semester at Sea, a program in which students take courses in history, political science, and geography while sailing around the world and stopping in several countries to travel and conduct research. At each port, an expert joins the ship to lecture about the country the students are about to visit.

The program was expensive, but Joe was already a semester ahead in his course load and had received a small scholarship. Furthermore, he convinced me this was the opportunity of a lifetime. I had always wanted to see Seattle and Vancouver, where the ship would depart, so I accompanied him to British Columbia in September of 1995 to see him off and arranged for him to fly back to Chicago from his last port in Fort Lauderdale the week before Christmas.

In his dispatches, Joe wrote about getting seasick as their ship barely avoided typhoons off the coast of Japan, that they were rerouted to Sri Lanka when a flu epidemic in India alarmed the captain, and what it was like to climb the Great Wall of China.

He was fascinated by Egypt and attended lectures on the prospect of peace in the Middle East as they sailed through the Suez Canal and docked at Haifa on the Israeli coast. When they reached Istanbul, Joe was asked to serve as the lecturer on Turkey, and he spoke about the Ottoman Empire and the Turkish Republic. They crossed the Black Sea and from Odessa flew to St. Petersburg in Russia and eventually sailed back through the Black Sea and the Mediterranean. Casablanca was their final stop before sailing for Florida at the end of the semester.

I was anxiously awaiting Joe's arrival in Chicago after three months of travel, when I received a phone call from the dean of his program at the tail end of their trip.

"Mrs. Yackley, I am calling about your son," he began. "I hate to be the bearer of bad news but Joe has been breaking many of the Semester at Sea rules. Unfortunately, we have no choice but to dismiss him from the program," he said.

My heart sank. This meant Joe would lose a whole semester of credit.

"But Joe is such a good student," I argued. "Didn't he do well in his classes?"

It seemed Joe hadn't been a model student after all. He had been violating a range of rules laid out in an agreement all students signed before enrolling. He had hitchhiked in the Philippines, rented motorbikes in Vietnam, and climbed the pyramids by moonlight in Egypt. On a couple of occasions he had returned to the ship, after the required time, just as it was set to sail. The final blow came in Morocco, when he was caught smuggling alcohol onto the ship.

I was finally able to speak with him as he arrived in Florida, and he was terribly upset. I heard tears in his voice. This unfortunate event would become an important turning point in Joe's life. He had planned to spend the remainder of his junior year with his aunt and uncle in Germany but was now forced to return to Evanston to make up his coursework.

Joe was down in the dumps for months, having lost his self-confidence until he began dating one of Ayla's sorority sisters. It was a close and loving relationship that would last five years, during which they each earned their master's degrees. Right after graduation, Joe moved to Hanover, where he studied at the university, improved his German and Turkish, developed an interest in Middle Eastern history, and found a sense of direction in his life. He returned to Chicago to earn two master's degrees at the University of Chicago.

Joe has published articles in German, Turkish, and American journals and lectured before a dozen international groups on various topics. He speaks five languages, has traveled to fifty different countries, and spent three or more months in a half-dozen nations. He now pursues a Ph.D. in Near Eastern Languages and Civilizations at the University of Chicago.

Frank was right when he wrote in his last letter to the children:

"I believe each of you will do very fine things in life and each in very different ways. I not only love you but I admire each of you so much – I look up to you, as one would ordinarily do only with older persons."

I am grateful Joe survived some tough times and thrived emotionally and intellectually. More and more, he reminds me of his dad, who was also an avid reader, a quiet, private, and reflective person. Joe's coloring, physique, eating habits, mental organization, love of physical activity, and need for eight hours of sleep all mirror Frank's qualities. He has adopted some of the habits of his father, like the way he eats an apple: stem, seeds, and all.

Unlike his Dad, Joe feels at home anywhere in the world, adaptable to the culture in which he finds himself.

I tell Joe, as well as John and Ayla, that they should share their thoughts, feelings, worries, and demons with loved ones. They should be pragmatic and accepting of the fact that bipolar illness has a genetic predisposition. They should seek help at the first sign of depression or unusual behavior. By talking about it and being well informed, they can help de-stigmatize mental illness and humanize it.

"If tears had not been shed or hearts burned by lovers, there would be neither water nor fire in the world."
– Mevlana Jalaluddin Rumi

18 - Sel's Challenges

The stress of the dozen years following Frank's suicide eventually took its toll on me. During the mid-1990s, I began feeling sad and exhausted. I had been full of energy all my life, so I attributed the change to long hours at work, the aging process, and the extra 15 pounds I was carrying around since menopause. Not wanting to cut off all ties with Ottawa, I had not found an internist or an optometrist in Chicago for sentimental reasons.

Working 10-hour days at Artun Travel, with a telephone cradled between my shoulder and my ear, was giving me a stiff back. Then I had trouble focusing my eyes on the computer screen and my right eyelid began to sag. A friend referred me to an ophthalmologist who diagnosed me with ptosis, a congenital condition in which the eyelid droops. The doctor listed a number of possible causes, including stress, overuse of the eyes, thyroid deficiency, an abrupt eye injury, or genetic tendencies. He later claimed he also mentioned myasthenia gravis, a rare autoimmune disease, as a possible cause.

"You must reduce the stress at work and rest your eyes often," he said. "Let's first rule out thyroid problems. I'll send you to an endocrinologist for some blood work."

The blood tests came back negative – no thyroid problems, no other suspicious causes – but the ptosis persisted. After several months, I decided to go to a neurologist, and a neighbor recommended a doctor at Northwestern Memorial Hospital who examined me thoroughly. He made me walk on my toes, squat and rise, resist his push on my fingers, arms, legs, feet, and forehead. "You seem to be in good shape. Just reduce your hours at work," he said.

Hoping I could live on Frank's pension, I decided to retire early and avoid further stress from my job at Artun Travel. I needed time to exercise and to relax. Within three months, and not yet 60 years old, I realized I needed more income.

Picasso Travel, a Turkish-owned travel consolidator, headquartered in Los Angeles, had branches in New York, Boston, and San Francisco and was looking for a manager to open an office in Chicago. They approached me with a very good offer, and the idea of managing and organizing an office from scratch appealed to me and energized me.

I discounted my persistent ailments and flew to Los Angeles to negotiate a good contract. In addition to my salary for managing the office, I would be paid commissions on any retail business I generated. The contract also stipulated that I would receive a substantial bonus after twelve months if we met the owner's sales targets. With such great incentives, I rolled up my sleeves and went to work.

I had no idea I had just entered the cutthroat world of corporate business.

As a manager, I dealt with building contractors configuring office space, hired and trained six employees, solicited business from travel agents, and met with airline representatives to negotiate attractive rates. The Chicago office was soon doing gangbuster business – beating the competition on several fronts, especially in selling to travel agents who catered to Polish and Middle Eastern clientele. Having worked in the travel business in Chicago for eight years previously gave me an edge with airlines, travel agents, and retail clients. I also made use of my writing skills and contacts and publicized the business in the *Chicago Tribune* and the trade journals.

I walked to work and back to stay in shape. Still, I lacked energy and fell into bed totally exhausted every night. The ptosis on my right eye worsened toward the end of the summer, at times interfering with my sight. One evening, driving from the suburbs after a long day, I caught myself putting my head farther back to see out of my right eye. When that did not work, I covered my right eye with my right hand, jeopardizing my driving ability.

Something had to be done about my sagging eyelid. I attended several workshops on plastic surgery and decided an eyelid lift was the answer. After much research, I chose Dr. David Teplica, a soft-spoken, attentive plastic surgeon. He pointed out that there are many causes for ptosis and that surgery might be only a temporary solution.

Still, on a sunny Thursday morning in August 1998, I underwent general anesthetic and had the surgery. I was to sleep on my back with pillows propping me up, a challenge for someone who sleeps on her side without a pillow. After three days of dry, scratchy eyes and little sleep, I returned to work, having taken off only two days. I wore glasses instead of contact lenses for the next six weeks, and people told me I looked great, well-rested, and wide-awake. The eyelid lift seemed to have taken a few years off my age.

In the meantime the travel business kept getting more competitive and less enjoyable.

Early in February, ten months after I launched the Midwest branch, I sensed tension building up in the office. The bookkeeper, a Turkish acquaintance who had been thrilled when I helped her re-enter the job market after a long absence, was no longer friendly. Instead of giving me the daily report, she was on the phone with the New York branch manager, who began to meddle in our day-to-day operations.

I was criticized for petty things such as the way I dispensed souvenirs brought to our office by the airlines. I was questioned about a lunch bill with an airline representative and a cab fare to visit a travel agency. Even though I was in the office before everyone else and left after they were gone, I was told I missed checking certain transactions and was not "supervising the staff closely." I knew something strange was going on, but I couldn't figure out what.

I finally confronted the owner, calling him in Los Angeles. He said Chicago was doing quite well, and then coyly added, "Maybe it can function without a manager on site." Without pausing, he said, "We don't want to lose you. You know a lot of people and do an excellent job with retail sales and public relations. You have great writing skills and wonderful connections."

Taking advantage of my shocked silence, he suggested I take on another role and admitted such a move would void my contract and result in a pay cut. So the recent nitpicking had been aimed at driving me away. In another month, I would have qualified for the bonus as stipulated in my contract. He wanted to demote me before my anniversary date to avoid paying the bonus.

He told me my options were to stay and work in retail sales, set up a home office and work as an outside agent, or handle Picasso's PR work as an independent contractor. None of these options was acceptable. I wanted nothing more to do with Picasso. "What if I leave?" I asked.

He offered me three months' salary, two business-class international tickets, and an open door if both sides agreed I should return. I packed up my belongings and left 11 months after I launched the branch. That May, I used one of the tickets on British Airways to visit John in Ireland on Mother's Day, then my sister in Germany. When Picasso refused to pay me the commissions for my retail sales, I hired a labor attorney and went to court. Eventually, I collected all monies owed me, and the judge made them pay the court costs.

Yet the additional stress resulted in a recurrence of the ptosis during the summer of 2000. My semi-annual visits to the neurologist, who was still seeking a cause, were inconclusive. He encouraged me to continue keeping my muscles strong, and on my fourth visit, he asked once again whether I was seeing double, which I was. He decided to revisit the possibility of myasthenia gravis and ordered a blood test. The doctor was alarmed by the result. My antibodies were hovering around 9.3 when the normal is 0.8. He then ordered a CAT scan that showed a growth on my thymus gland, which controls the immune system. Pea-sized when we are born, the thymus shrinks to a small spot as we grow older. Mine was one by two centimeters, quite large. This development confirmed the diagnosis; I had myasthenia gravis.

My friend Linda Andrews accompanied me to the doctor's office, taking notes and asking a lot of questions. A faculty member at the University of Illinois at Chicago, she had access to the university's medical databases and provided me with a great deal of facts about MG.

I have kept all sorts of information in a thick three-ring binder, and the more I know about this chronic illness, the less I fear it. The immune system normally protects the body from foreign organisms, but with MG patients, the immune system mistakenly attacks itself. It is a rare disease, affecting three out of 10,000 people, including women of childbearing age or men 70 years or older.   The most famous sufferer was the late Greek shipping magnate Aristotle Onasis.

Treatment has not changed much since the 1930s.   Drug therapy is required, and I take three Mestinon tablets a day to avoid extreme fatigue and double vision.   Some patients have to be on Imuran or Prednisone, if Mestinon does not work for them.

With Linda's help, I discovered Dr. Matthew Merrigiolli, a neurologist specializing in MG who sits on the board of the Chicago-based National Myasthenia Gravis Foundation.   Dr. Merrigiolli also served as director of an MG clinic at Rush Presbyterian St. Luke's Hospital.

Under his care, I went through more blood tests, another CAT scan, and a computerized test with needles in my arm and leg muscles, checking the connection between my muscles and nerve endings.   Dr. Merrigiolli came up with a similar diagnosis and said the tumor on the thymus gland probably was not malignant but that surgery might improve my autoimmune system and antibody count.   Once I decided in favor of surgery I wanted to get it over with right away, even though I had no family close by.   John was working in Dublin, Ayla was in Turkey, and Joe was taking courses at Hanover University in Germany.   Friends came through once again, several volunteering to take me to the hospital, others planning to stay with me once I returned home.

Still, John was determined to be at my side during the surgery. He made last-minute arrangements to fly to Chicago from Dublin. His trip, however, caused me more anxiety than my upcoming surgery.   A delayed take-off in Dublin resulted in a missed connection in Paris, which caused a late arrival at JFK airport in New York, with no more flights to Chicago available that night. My Turkish friend Emel Singer took me to Rush at 7 a.m. and stayed until John met me in the recovery room three hours later. His 24-hour journey and concern about my health seemed to have aged him.   Nevertheless, he knew how much I appreciated his heroic efforts.

He kept everyone informed about my progress and brought me home after three days. Ayhan Lash, another Turkish friend and a professor of nursing, stayed with me for a few days, so John felt comfortable going back to his job in Dublin.

Although it took two years to notice a slight improvement in my double vision and fatigue, Dr. Merrigiolli was right. If I don't take my medication on time or succumb to stress, the symptoms return. The doctor tells me I have to keep my muscles strong, so I exercise on the treadmill and with resistance-training machines, take Pilates classes, and do laps at the swimming pool.

My condition frustrates me since I've been on the go all my life. I want to continue learning, writing, traveling, networking, and socializing. I try to keep my MG under control by eating properly, exercising, getting enough sleep, and taking my medication and vitamins. I supplement my income from Social Security and Frank's pension with freelance writing and travel work, which I enjoy.

Settled into my two-bedroom apartment on Chicago's Gold Coast, I became more involved with the Turkish community, which nicknamed me "Mama Turk" because I take under my wing students from Turkey in order to help them experience a smooth adjustment to the American way of life. I remember my humble beginnings in this country and find strength in helping those in similar situations.

I volunteered to help raise funds to establish an Ottoman professorship at the University of Chicago and support archeological excavations undertaken in Turkey by the university's Oriental Institute. I thrive on tackling projects for the International Women Associates and enjoy organizing fundraisers, seminars, speakers' bureaus, and tours of Turkey.

I like participating in various medical research projects and have volunteered for hormone-therapy studies at the Women's Health Center at Rush Presbyterian St. Luke's Medical Center for 10 years. Being closely monitored as a study subject resulted in the early discovery of an ovarian cyst. This time Joe was back in Chicago and brought me home after the outpatient procedure.

I also participated in some research studies that were uncomfortable, even painful. One of these was the four-day sleep study at Northwestern Memorial Hospital in which I was confined to a dimly lit room and blood samples were taken from my arm every four hours. Something positive came out of this adventure: I got into the habit of going to bed at the same time each evening.

My children know that I do not want to be on life support if I become incompetent and terminally ill. And I've signed papers to donate my body to science after my death; my brain goes to Northwestern Memorial Hospital's Alzheimer's research department, where I have been a control subject since 2001, undergoing memory tests and brain MRIs.

My friends tease me because I let my hair grow at least 10 inches in between haircuts so I can donate it to Locks of Love, a non-profit group that makes human-hair wigs for people who have lost their hair, mostly during chemotherapy for cancer.

I'm not sure why I participate in the medical studies or jump through such hoops to help those who are suffering. It may seem macabre to some. Perhaps I need to be needed. If so, did I become this way twenty three years ago when Frank became sick and I had to be strong? Have I fully dealt with the grief of losing Frank? Have I made peace with myself?

I do not have answers to these questions. All I know is that after two decades of ups and downs, I am overjoyed to know that John, Ayla, and Joe are each other's best friends, looking to one another for support and advice. They are strong and sturdy, meeting life's challenges with determination. They are educated, productive, compassionate adults.

I am touched by their concern for my health, heed their criticism of my over-commitments, and listen to their nagging that I reduce the stress in my life. I am flattered by their need for my approval of the choices they make in their careers and in other aspects of their lives. I welcome their amusement when I, a non-native English speaker, mispronounce a word or use the wrong idiom. I cherish their hugs when they are near and their declarations of love when they are far.

Ten years ago, the four of us journeyed back to Ottawa to close a chapter in our lives together. For years, my kids had persuaded me to postpone the sale of our home on Congress Street where they had grown up, but the time had come for another family to make it their own. My children had moved on, and now it was my turn.

That handsome brick house – with its screened-in porch, stately maple and oak trees, whitewashed window frames, and ivy-covered exterior – had become a warehouse of memories of their youthful selves and of their father. The basement still had his workshop, the closets contained his clothes. On the wood floor of our family room, drops of Frank's sweat, which fell from his brow as he refinished the house in 1971, had been preserved beneath the varnish. Dull etchings on the doorjamb of the kitchen marked the height of each child on every one of his or her birthdays. In their bedrooms, secret doodlings on the corners of walls contained messages that were once all-important: "Ayla Loves Scott," "Joe and Aaron – Best Friends Forever," or John's signature tag, "Chicken Sauce Was Here."

Together we sorted through a quarter-century of our accumulations. I salvaged photo albums, a few of Frank's favorite books, and the mandolin he had unsuccessfully petitioned me to play during his campaign. Joe grabbed the miniature NFL helmets he had collected from cereal boxes in the 1970s. John picked out my ancient steamer trunk and the rocking chair on which I had nursed him as an infant. Ayla, dressed in one of my old wool sweaters, snapped photos of blank walls, empty closets, bare cupboards. All three ceremoniously threw away their countless trophies and ribbons and medals in a giant red dumpster outside. Their final act before we turned the keys over was to go from one room to another, now all vacant, and share their memories of each space.

As the new owners milled about inside, I stood on the back porch and watched John, Ayla, and Joe play a last game of pick-up basketball in the driveway. Love surged through me as I beheld the two boys and the girl Frank had given me. I pressed my eyes shut and heard their laughter, the ball bouncing off concrete, the birdsong from our peach trees, and I did not regret the pain.

> **"The great thing in this world is not where we stand,
> but in what direction we are moving."**
> – Oliver Wendell Holmes

Case Histories and Further Information

Every year as many as 15 million Americans suffer from major depression and bipolar disorder, the most common forms of mental illness. If undiagnosed or untreated, suicide might become a desperate option for these sufferers.

Just before going to press with this book, we were traumatized by another suicide – that of 22-year-old Jack Breslin, the tall, handsome, quiet, and sensitive son of Peg and John. "He could no longer bear the weight of the cross he was carrying," eulogized his uncle, Father Peter Breslin.   Jack's aunt, Sister Maureen McDonnell, offered these prayers:

"We pray for those who are doing research and treatment to heal and improve the lives of the mentally ill so that their work may bear fruit; for all who live with mental illness, that they be understood and accepted more fully and appreciated for the many gifts they offer to society; for families affected by mental illness, that they may find strength and patience that they need."

An article in the *Chicago Tribune* in January 2006 quoted a survey of 600 bipolar patients who said they had seen an average of four physicians and received three misdiagnoses before they were accurately diagnosed. Such misdiagnosis results in a gap averaging more than 10 years between onset of the disease and treatment.

"The diagnosis you get determines the treatment you get, and the treatment you get might determine how well you are able to live with your disorder," writes author Lori Oliwenstein in *Taming Bipolar Disorder.*

Dozens of books on bipolar illness such as *Surviving Manic Depression* by Dr. Torrey and Michael B. Knable, D.O, have been published in the last two decades. These doctors tell us to be proactive with our loved ones who are experiencing depression by asking them some direct questions.

Are you thinking of harming yourself?

Do you have a plan to do so?

What preparations have you made to carry out such a plan?

"The next step should be taking away the means of committing suicide, such as pills and weapons. Then notify the psychiatrist, request hospitalization (voluntary or involuntary) and act as if this is an emergency," the authors say. Torrey and Knable concede that despite best efforts by family members and professionals, some individuals with manic depression will commit suicide. If family and friends have done all they could, they should not feel guilty or blame themselves. Instead they should seek help with their grief process. The American Association of Suicidology has a helpful database of support groups listed by state. For literature and fact sheets go to its Website www.suicidology.org.

Suicide is the 11th leading cause of death in the United States, resulting in more than 30,000 fatalities each year, according to the Centers for Disease Control and Prevention. The American Association of Suicidology, which studies suicide and suicide prevention, says every 16 minutes a person dies by suicide in the United States. In Illinois more people die from suicide than homicide. Individually or collectively, we must prevent this desperate last step, especially among young people. We need the kind of funding for research and treatment of mental illness on a par with the monies raised for cancer, diabetes, heart disease, and Alzheimer's research.

Dr. Jan Fawcett's book *New Hope for People with Bipolar Disorder* says: "The deeply depressed state of mind, all pervasive as it seems to the sufferer, can be completely lifted and held at bay by successful treatment. Doctors see this happen many times, and it is an amazing miracle to behold."

Information about manic depression and mental illness come from many varied sources.

Actress Patty Duke has shared her story in *A Brilliant Madness: Living with Manic Depressive Illness*, and *Call Me Anna*. She recently started a blog enabling people affected by the illness to chat with each other.

Television personality Jane Pauley made public the details of her bipolar illness in her book *Skywriting: Life Out of the Blue* and in numerous interviews on television and radio.

The book and Oscar-winning movie *A Beautiful Mind* about Nobel Prize winner John Nash made us aware of how extremely intelligent minds can cross the line into madness.

Fallout, a play by writer and director Todd Logan, draws from his life as he presented an honest portrayal of how mental illness can affect a family. "The toughest thing about being a family member of a mentally ill person is accepting the fact that our loved one is not the person we knew before he/she got sick," Logan says.

Support groups can make a big difference and the Internet has a great deal of information on bipolar disorder and how to cope with it.

Since Frank's death, I have spoken at various meetings and counseling sessions. I hear similar heart-breaking stories from families struggling with bipolar illness. At a mental health clinic in Central Illinois, a group of witty, coherent people shared their stories with me. They knew a great deal about mental illness but were frustrated and impatient with their situations.

Marilyn came from a family of ten adult children, seven suffering from bipolar disorder. This tall, husky-voiced 50-something woman's somber face reflected sadness to her core. With her blonde hair gathered on the top of her head and her blue eyes showing signs of anger, she said, "I have been trying various medications and different doctors for the last 15 years, but I cannot shake the hopelessness and feelings of doom." She admitted she tried to kill herself on three separate occasions.

Robert, a tired looking, sad-eyed gentleman, related how delusional and unpredictable his wife becomes when she does not take her medication. "How can I force an adult in her 40s, to take her medicine?" he asked. "How can I take care of her and keep the rest of the family functioning normally? My wife has been in and out of the hospital for the last three years. She is okay for a few weeks after she gets home. Pretty soon, she quits taking her medicine and goes into a manic state, from which she crashes. She crashes so hard that I have to take her back to the hospital."

A heavy-set, unkempt man in his early 30s, who looked a great deal older, said he was suffering from the "FBI syndrome." He ranted and raved about people watching him and was sure the government was out to get him. The counselor later confirmed he was a paranoid schizophrenic.

A young African-American with a great physique and a friendly smile shared his story. During his late teens he was drinking and doing drugs. After getting into trouble with the law, he was finally diagnosed as a manic-depressive. "I am lucky I did not continue on that other path," he said as he patted his mother's knee.

His middle-aged mother with braided hair and keen eyes said she had earned a college degree, like most of her other children. "But my life has added up to zero," she said. "I did not know what was wrong with me. I could not hold down a job for more than a couple of months and I could not keep from drinking and acting out." The doctor who diagnosed her son's illness discovered she

193

was also bipolar. "He put me on medication that is working very well, but I cannot drink any alcohol at all," she said. The son interrupted to say, "The doctor tells me I can drink a couple of drinks if I want to." Several people in the group chided him, telling him alcohol is a depressant and that he was interfering with the positive effects of the medicine when he drank.

A gray-haired lady in her 70s, who had entered the room with the help of a walker, kept easing closer and closer to her husband as others talked. He introduced himself and said, "I am here because I want to learn how to better understand my wife's illness and be more of a help to her." Looking at him with adoring eyes, she said, "I am so lucky to have him. I was in and out of hospitals for years, lonely and lost before he came into my life. He keeps me sane and balanced."

While I was writing this book, I learned that Frank's niece and our bridesmaid, Kathy Rackley, was diagnosed with manic depression. She led a gypsy-like life as a young adult. Married and divorced twice, she was first diagnosed with seasonal depression and moved to sunnier climates to help alleviate this problem but did not seek further medical help until recently. Unfortunately, she has no medical insurance and worries the medication is not working. She is not impressed with her doctor. I urge her to be patient and tell her that with time, proper drugs and medical attention will ease her pain. "I am sticking with my medication, but it is so hard," she emailed me recently. "Even with the medication, I have such negative thoughts all the time. Who would have thought this illness would be the curse of the Yackley family?"

A young woman who works in John's office struggled with terrible bipolar episodes that forced her to be hospitalized. "Seeking a therapist and taking medication is essential for bipolar people to remain stable," she says. "It takes a while for a doctor to find the right 'cocktail' of medications, which is why people relapse so much. It took two years for me to be balanced."

Unfortunately this young lady relapsed recently after six years of being fine. She admitted she was stretching her "meds and not taking them regularly, just so they would last longer." Luckily her insurance covered the three weeks of relapse hospitalization, and her employer gave her the time to recover. "Needless to say, I learned my lesson and am taking my medicine regularly and will continue taking it until the day I die," she says, accepting the truth of her illness.

A highly intelligent friend has been collecting disability because he is in no condition to hold a job, but he refuses medical treatment, instead choosing holistic "cures" for his paranoia. He copes well for a while but relapses into psychotic episodes that frustrate his friends and family. He insists his troubles began with a severe trauma to the head suffered during a motorcycle accident, which is possible. Like Frank and his niece, there is history of mental illness in his family.

The fatal shooting of Rigoberto Alpizar at the Miami International Airport in December 2005 demonstrates how vital it is for a bipolar person to take his medication. Alpizar, a U.S. citizen, and a missionary, arriving from Colombia, South America on an American Airlines flight, was shot five times by federal marshals because he was acting belligerently. He allegedly claimed he had a bomb in his bag and would not stop when the marshals ordered him to do so. His despondent wife later told the authorities he was acting erratically because he had not been taking his medication.

As Jane Pauley writes in *Skywriting*, the first step is accepting the diagnosis. The next step is medication along with therapy under the supervision of a doctor you like and trust.

"I have suffered depression since I was 27 and was diagnosed with bipolar disorder at age 32," says Ron, who is now 58. "Thank God I am in control of my illness. My secret to living a 'normal' life is the following," listing the points on Patty Duke's blog site:

Stay on proper medication and attend sessions with a good therapist.

Practice cognitive behavior theory.

Exercise at least three or four days a week (break into sweat).

Join a support group.

Try your best to feel good about yourself.

We know the biggest risk factor is genetics, as described in *Surviving Manic Depression* by Dr. E. Fuller Torrey and Michael B. Knable.

"How Strong Is the Evidence?"

Genes	very strong
Winter birth	strong
Summer onset	strong
Urban birth	weak
Pregnancy and birth complications	moderate
Prenatal exposure to influence	negative
Severe stressors in childhood	moderate
Physical or sexual abuse	weak
Loss of parent	weak
Head injuries	
within five years of onset	moderate
in childhood	weak
Social class	moderate

In early 2006, Australian researchers found that those with a gene linked to being bipolar, or manic-depressive, are twice as likely to develop the disease. Scientists at the Garvan Institute of Medical Research in Sydney and University of New South Wales discovered the first risk gene specifically for bipolar disorder. "We are the first group in the world to take a multi-faceted approach to identify a bipolar risk gene – we used a number of families, unrelated patients, and therapeutic drug mouse models.

Each of these three lines of investigation led us to a gene called FAT," said lead author Dr. Ian Blair.

Now that I know several generations in Frank's family have suffered from psychological disorders, I am quick to admit that my husband had mood swings when I first met him. However, the onset of his full-blown illness and correct diagnosis came late, after he turned 46. Treatment methods were limited in the early 1980s. Like many other highly intelligent people, he thought he could deal with his illness without medicine and therapy. There are so many medical advances now.

My advice is simple, amateur, and humble:

- Do not be ashamed of admitting you or a family member suffers mental illness.

- Help your partner or family member shop around for the best specialist. If you do not bond with one medical professional, seek out another one.

- Ask for the latest treatment programs. For example, doctors recently implanted a pacemaker in one patient's chest that supplies the correct amount of chemicals to her brain to enable her to live a normal, contented life.

- If you are worried or suspicious that your offspring may have a similar disorder, get them tested to help determine whether they have bipolar or other mental problems. This will give you a chance to preempt the illness.

- Read and learn as much as you can. Understand the pain that is crippling the victim.

- Do not keep the illness a secret. Open discussion helps the healing process. The more you talk about the illness, the easier it becomes to accept and deal with it.

- Support groups, mental health counselors, hospitals, clinics and doctors are there to help.

- Share your story and listen to the suffering of others. You are not alone. Enlist the support of your family and friends.
- Share your experiences with hundreds of others. Seek comfort from websites such as www.pattyduke.net and talk to others through her recently created blog. You can stay totally anonymous in your discussions. Try pattydukeblog@googlegroups.com.
- Remember bipolar illness is physiological just as diabetes, congestive heart trouble or autoimmune diseases are. With improved medications, new treatment methods and effective support groups, no one should feel helpless or hopeless.

Geniuses like Aristotle, William Wadsworth, Fredrick Nietzsche, and Ralph Waldo Emerson all suffered from bipolar illness, according to Jan Fawcett, M.D. but could not have known what made them so miserable. Many, including Vincent Van Gogh, Fredrick Chopin, and Ernest Hemingway, chose to end their lives.

Then there are present-day celebrities like Patty Duke, Mike Wallace, and Jane Pauley, who are living productive and inspirational lives. We should be grateful for the advances made in diagnosis and treatment of mental illnesses and demand continued research.

It is my sincere hope that this book enlightens readers and helps family members cope with this chronic ailment.

This is why I wrote it.

"The greatest gifts you can give our children are the roots of responsibility and the wings of independence."
– Denis Waitley

Epilogue

I have never regretted my decision to marry Frank and support his ambitions in his legal career. I took as much pride in his accomplishments as he did. We had twenty wonderful, loving years together even though there were rocky periods and unmet needs during some of that time. He was charming, brilliant, and caring before his bipolar illness. He was also unpredictable, but I had learned to adjust to that.

The last three years of his life were difficult, but I was prepared to stand by him. If Frank had been less rigid, more open to seeking other doctors' opinions, and willing to experiment with different medicines, he might still be here.

Frank's legacy is all around us. I see it in John's sense of humor, Ayla's love for the written word, and Joe's athletic build and scholarly ways. I pray that the genetic predisposition toward bipolar illness does not show up in my children.

My goal was to help each of them become levelheaded, compassionate, intelligent, self-reliant, responsible, and loving adults. I believe I have helped them do so. I am thankful for the opportunities that enabled me to live in and adapt to two cultures, receive a good education and earn a living, marry and raise children, and cultivate numerous friendships that have, in turn, sustained me.

My hope has been to write a book that would reach out to those who face the challenges of bipolar illness and give them hope and courage.

Recommended Reading and Resources

Books:

Abbas, Jen, *Generation Ex: Adult Children of Divorce and the Healing of Our Pain, 2004*

Amador, Xavier and Johanson, Anna-Lisa. *I Am Not Sick, I Don't Need Help! Helping the Seriously Mentally Ill Accept Treatment,* 2000

Basco, Monica Ramirer, *The Bipolar Workbook: Tools for Controlling Your Mod Swings,* 2005

Basco, Monica Ramirez and Rush, John A, *Cognitive-Behavioral Therapy for Bipolar Disorder, Second Edition, 2005*

Burns, D. David, *Feeling Good: The New Mood Therapy,* 1999.

Castle, Lana R, Whybrow, Peter, *Bipolar Disorder Demystified: Mastering the Tightrope of Manic Depression,* 2003

Duke, Patty and Kenneth Turan, *Call Me Anna,* 1987

Duke, Patty and Gloria Hochman, *A Brilliant Madness,* 1992

Fast, Julie A. and Preston, John D., *Loving Someone with Bipolar Disorder,* 2004

Fawcett, Jan, Golden, Bernard, Rosenfeld, Rosenfeld, *New Hope for People with Bipolar Disorder,* 2000

Never Regret the Pain: Loving and Losing a Bipolar Spouse

Fieve, Ronald, M.D. *Mood Swings*, 1982

Fink, Candida and Kraynak Joe, Bipolar Disorder for Dummies, *2005*

Fristad, Mary A, and Goldberg Arnold Jill, *Raising a Model Child: How to Cope with Depression and Bipolar Disorder*, 2003

Granet, Roger, Feber, Elizabeth, *Why Am I Up, Why Am I Down?*, 1999

Hamer, Dean, Copeland, Peter, *Living with Our Genes*, 1999

Jamison, Kay Redfield, *An Unquiet Mind: Memoir of Moods and Madness*, 1995

Jamison, Kay Redfield, *Touched with Fire: Manic Depressive Illness and the Artistic Temperament*, 1996

Jamison, Kay Redfield, *Night Falls Fast: Understanding Suicide*, 2000

Marohn, Stephanie. *The Natural Medicine Guide to Bipolar Disorder (The Healthy Mind Guides)*, 2003

Miller, Linda Lael, *Never Look Back, 2005*

Miklowitz, David. *The Bipolar Disorder Survival Guide: What Your and Your Family Need to Know*, 2002

Mondimore, Francis Mark, M.D. *Bipolar Disorder: A Guide for Patients and Families*, 1999

Moyer, David, *Too Good to be True? Nutrients Quiet the Unquiet Brain—A four Generation Bipolar Odyssey, 2004*

Oliwenstein, Lori, *Taming Bipolar Disorder*, 2004

Pauley, Jane, *Skywriting: A Life Out of the Blue,* Random House, 2004

Rayel, Michael G. M.D., *First Aid to Mental Illness: A Practical Guide for Patients and Caregivers,* Soar Dime Ltd, 2004

Torrey, E. Fuller, and Knable, Michael, *Surviving Manic Depression*, Basic Books, 2002

Vine, Phyllis, *Families in Pain,* Pantheon Books, 1982

Whybrow, Peter C. M.D., *A Mood Apart: Depression, Mania, and Other Afflictions of the Self*, Perennial, 1998

Worthen, Mary. *Journey Not Chosen...Destination Not Known,* August House Publishers, 2001

Goodwin F K, Jamison, Kay, Redfield, *70 Signs of Depression: Recognize and Cope With Our Loved One's Clinical or Manic-Depressive Illness,* Oxford University Press, 1990

Articles:

Brune, Adrian. "Changing Minds: Surgeons Step in When Pills and Therapy Fail," *Chicago Tribune Magazine*, Apr. 24, 2005

Gunderson, Bolton S. "Distinguishing Borderline Personality Disorder from Bipolar Disorder," *American Journal of Psychiatry 1996*

Winokur G, Coryell W, Endicott J. "Further Distinctions Between Manic-depressive Illness (bipolar disorder) and Primary Depressive Disorder (unipolar depression)" *American Journal of Psychiatry* 1993

Dunner D.L., Patrick V., Fieve, R.R., "Rapid-cycling Manic Depressive Patients" *Comparative Psychiatry* 1977

Goleman, Daniel, "Understanding the Painful Path that Leads to Suicide." *New York Times News Service*, Mar. 15, 2003

Levine, Irene S. "The Secret is out—finally" *Chicago Tribune Q-Section*, January 15, 2006

Rayel, Michael G., M.D., "How Do You Know If You Have Manic Depression", *Christian Mommies,* 2004

Web Sites:

www.bipolarhome.org
www.psychiatry24x7.com
www.bpkids.org
www.managingbipolar.com
www.bipolarworld.net
www.medicinenet.com/bipolar
http://www.bipolarhappens.com/
http://www.bipolarcentral.com
http://www.BipolarSupporter.com
http://www.mhsanctuary.com/bipolar/
http://www.DBSAlliance.org
http://www.bipolar.big.com
http://www.depressionhurts.com
http://www.bipolarmaniainfo.com
http://www.truehope.com
http://www.afsp.org
http://www.cabf.org
http://www.nmha.org

Online center for mental wellness
www.pattyduke.net

Mental Wellness Centers:

National Alliance for the Mentally Ill
National Institute of Mental Health
WebMD Bipolar Info Center
BiPolar.about.com
Depression and Bipolar Support Alliance
Focus Adolescent Services
Washington University School of Medicine Collaborative Genomic Study of Bipolar Disorder

About the Author

Sel Erder Yackley is an award-winning journalist who was born and reared in Turkey. After receiving her master's degree in journalism from Northwestern University in Evanston, Illinois, she worked for United Press International (where she met Frank) and for the *Chicago Tribune.* During the 1970s, while raising their three children, Sel became active in local politics as well as civic and charitable organizations in central Illinois. Ten years after her husband's suicide she returned to Chicago to work in the travel business and became involved in mental health issues. On the boards of several international groups, Sel continues to write, organize tours to Turkey, and lectures at support groups.

Visit Sel at http://www.selyackley.com

06

Printed in the United States
99113LV00003B/237/A